Entrepreneur
MAGAZINE'S

PROJECT MANAGEMENT

made easy

Entrepreneur Press and
Sid Kemp

EP Entrepreneur Press

Editorial Director: Jere Calmes
Cover Design: Beth Hansen-Winter
Editorial and Production Services: CWL Publishing Enterprises, Inc., Madison,
Wisconsin, www.cwlpub.com

This is a CWL Publishing Enterprises book developed for Entrepreneur Press by
CWL Publishing Enterprises, Inc., Madison, Wisconsin.

ISBN 1-932531-77-7

Library of Congress Cataloging-in-Publication Data

Kemp, Sid.
  Project management for small business made easy / by Sid Kemp.
    p. cm.
  ISBN 1-932531-77-7 (alk. paper)
  1. Project management. 2. Small business--Management. I. Title.
  HD69.P75K4552 2006
  658.4'04--dc22

                                                                  2005030986

10 09 08 07 06 05   10 9 8 7 6 5 4 3 2 1

Printed in Canada

For Kris, my wife,

**who has stood by me as I've started
my own business, struggled,
succeeded, and found joy.**

Contents

Preface

Small Business Success

IS IT POSSIBLE TO DO GOOD WORK, SUCCEED, AND ENJOY THE PROCESS? *I'VE* found that owning or working for a small business can be challenging, rewarding, and fun all at once. It isn't always—and when the stuff hits the fan, the fun is the first thing to go. But if we learn how to get organized and stay on top of things, it can be an exciting ride with big rewards along the way and at the end.

Because I run my own business, I've had the chance to work with bright, creative, capable people. I've gotten to travel all over the country, try new things, and write books. Is your business giving you the opportunities you want? Are you realizing your dreams?

However much you are enjoying your work and succeeding, *Project Management for Small Business Made Easy* can help you do it more. As I wrote this book, one idea kept coming up over and over again, like a music theme in a movie: *eliminate hassle.* Learning and applying project management tools will help you eliminate hassles like these:

- ▶ You do a job, then find out it wasn't what the customer wanted.
- ▶ You give a job to a team member, but he or she forgets or misunderstands, and the work doesn't get done.
- ▶ Certain jobs are a pain in the anatomy, but you don't see how they can be fixed, so you just live with them over and over.

▶ Jobs simply take too long, so work piles up.

▶ Jobs cost too much, so you lose money.

▶ Everything seems to be going fine or things are just a bit off, and then, *bam!*—too much has gone wrong and the deadline is missed.

▶ Unexpected problems keep popping up.

▶ You can't seem to communicate your enthusiasm for your business to your team. You know if they cared the way you do, they'd be great, but they aren't invested, so the company just can't get any momentum going.

Project management is easy and it solves small business problems.

For all these different small business problems—and many others as well—project management is the solution. Most businesspeople think project management is either complicated or irrelevant. It's neither. It's simple and relevant. In fact, project management includes simple tools that solve small business problems.

Here are some key points that make project management really simple and valuable:

▶ *Any dream, opportunity, or problem can become a project.* So project management is the way to realize your dreams, seize opportunities, and solve problems.

▶ *Project management cuts big things down to size.* If you have a big challenge—you know, the one you keep putting off, hoping it will go away even though you know it won't—make it a project and cut it into pieces. Gather information, make plans, do the work, and the problem will be solved a lot sooner than you think.

▶ *Project management works for everyone.* If you or someone who works for you is having problems getting work done on time, or taking care of simple tasks, or learning to do something new, project management tools here in *Project Management for Small Business Made Easy* can help you cut through that problem, manage your work, and get things done.

▶ *Project management makes order out of chaos.* Sometimes, we are overwhelmed and things get out of control. In *Project Management for Small Business Made Easy*, you'll learn what it means to bring things under management, bring things under control. And you'll learn how to do it.

▶ *Project management is easy to learn.* It's a mix of common sense, sound thinking, and getting work done step by step. In fact, there are some natural project managers out there. (You'll learn about one in Chapter 21.) But project management is just like baseball. A natural can become a great pitcher. But anyone with some skills and desire can learn to toss a ball, have fun, and get the ball to the person who needs to catch it. You'll learn to toss products to your customers, they'll catch them, and they'll like what they get.

It is less expensive to solve a problem once than to live with it forever.

This book will help you with whatever dreams, opportunities, or problems you have in your business, whether you own it, work as a manager, or are on the team as an employee. It will help you get work done right and it will help your business make more money, satisfy more customers, clear away problems, and grow.

How to Use This Book

I've put this book together as 22 short, powerful chapters that each give you all you need on just one topic. Many of the chapters take less than half an hour to read. Each chapter presents just a few key ideas, so you'll be able to understand, retain, and use these practical tips and tools easily.

Chapters 1 to 5 talk about what a project is, what it means to bring something under management, and how to turn a dream, an opportunity, or a problem into a project that will be completed by a clear date that you set as a realistic goal. When you finish the first five chapters, you can pick a project and then work on it as you read the rest of the book.

Each project is organized into three stages: prepare, do, and follow-through.

You'll learn all about planning and preparation in Chapters 6 through 12. If you work on a project as you read, then, by the end of chapter 12, you'll have a thorough, complete, and clear plan and you'll be all ready to go.

Chapters 13 through 18 will take your project through the *doing stage*. You'll keep work, time, cost, and risk under control and deliver high-quality results step by step until everything is done. Then in Chapters 19 and 20, you'll learn the art of following through to customer delight. That's right: we project managers do more than satisfy our customers; we delight them. We meet or exceed expectations, we deliver what the customer wants, we express genuine care for our customers and concern for their goals, and we make up for mistakes with a bit of flair.

You don't need to be perfect. You just need to learn how to manage mistakes.

Chapters 21 and 22 are two bonuses. Chapter 21 is a case study of a very successful owner of two coffee shops that serve artisan-roasted coffee. You'll learn how the owners opened four businesses in six years, realizing their own dreams, delighting customers, and providing excellent opportunities for their employees by seizing opportunities and solving problems one after another. And in Chapter 22, you'll learn how to plan the projects for your own business, lining up a year of problem solving and business growth.

If you know how nails work, you can try pounding them with a rock or your shoe. However, it's easier and more effective and efficient to sink a nail with a hammer. Similarly, it's a lot easier to use project management ideas with tools and forms. At the back of the book, you'll find a section full of forms and tools that will make it easy to put all of *Project Management for Small Business Made Easy* to work. If you want these forms on full-sized sheets, plus a whole lot more, they are a free download away at www.qualitytechnology.com/DoneRight.

As you learn project management and do your next project, I'll be with you every step of the way. I know the journey will be rewarding. Make it fun, too!

Learning Project Management Is a Project

If you want to get the most out of this book, then make a project of learning project management. Commit to a goal: "I will be a better project manager by _____ (date)." Start reading, make a plan, and stay focused on learning project management so that you can eliminate hassles and succeed.

Chapter 1

Get It Done Right!

THIS CHAPTER ASKS THE QUESTION: HOW CAN A SMALL BUSINESS succeed in a rapidly changing world, with changing customer desires, new competitors, new technology, and new suppliers hitting us from all directions? The answer is project management. Project management helps us realize our dreams, take advantage of opportunities, and solve our problems in changing times. We'll put project management into simple language and learn how we can make projects work.

Small Business in a Changing World

If you own a small business, like I do, or if you work for one, you know that success depends on doing the right thing and on getting it done right. We need to deliver the right results, on time, and within our budget and do a really good job. When we do that over and over, we please our customers, we make money, and our business grows. When we don't get it done right—this may sound obvious—either we get it done wrong or we don't get it done at all. Then our customers aren't happy and our bank accounts are soon empty.

Small business owners have to deal with change, and good project management is the key to successful change.

Some jobs we do over and over. We stock up supplies, we make a sale, we balance the checkbook. We can think of these repetitive tasks as *production work*. But—unless you run a mom-and-pop grocery store—a lot of your work is done only once. The work is unique: decide what to stock for this season, negotiate a deal with one big client, arrange for a loan to open a new office or store. An MBA or any other standard business course won't help you do a good job at these unique, special jobs. Doing unique work and succeeding takes project management.

If our world—our customers, our suppliers, and our competitors—didn't change much, we wouldn't need much project management. But these days, everything is changing very fast. When I was growing up, there were no computers and almost nothing was made of plastic. More people used butter than margarine and no one knew about cholesterol. Music came on black vinyl albums played on phonographs. The only Teflon was on NASA spacecraft and the only product that came out of NASA's efforts was Tang® orange drink mix. Now we live in an era of microchips, microwaves, digital music, artificial foods, and microwave dinners. Our parents ate the same food throughout their entire lives; our children are eating new foods every few years.

But it's not just technology and products that are changing. Communication and transportation are faster and cheaper than ever before. Big business and franchises have taken over a lot of the commercial market. People expect products and services right away, and we can deliver because internet ordering has become part of how we do business.

If we can keep up.

And keeping up means dealing with change. It means setting new directions, revising our plans, and then getting new products, services, and ways of working in place quickly, before things change again.

Given how much things change, isn't it nice to know that there is a whole special field within business designed just to deal with change? It's called *project management*. The field has been growing for the last 35 years, and you can learn from the best and make it your own with *Project Management for Small Business Made Easy*.

What Is a Project?

A project is:

▶ A dream with a deadline

▶ A problem scheduled for solution

Do you have a dream for your business? Do you:

▶ Want to start a new business?

▶ Want to open a new location?

▶ Want to grow to a certain size?

▶ Want to be the best at what you do?

When you know what your dreams are, you know what your problems are.

Small Dreams Are OK, Too

A dream or opportunity doesn't have to be big. After all the trouble in 2001—the fall of the World Trade Center, the burst of the dotcom bubble, and Enron's scam—all of my clients didn't have enough money to pay me for a while. My dream for 2003—stay in business! Keep my company open! I managed that and, in 2004, I chose another small dream—make a little money this year! After that, I was ready for a big dream—write three books in 2005.

The lesson: Your dreams don't need to be big; they just need to be right for you right now. Do what works for you and your business.

If you're not sure, then ask, "What is the biggest opportunity for my business?"

When you've defined your dream or your opportunity, then you've set direction. When you've set direction, you head out on the road—and bam! You run into roadblocks. You want to hire more staff, but you can't find good people, you don't have room for them, and you're worried that you won't be able to keep up with the payroll come August, when the summer slump hits.

Each dream with a deadline or an opportunity we want to realize is a project. And that project defines the problems we face. And when we face those problems and solve them, that's a project, too.

Projects come in all sizes. In a small business, some might take months—such as launching the business or opening a new store. Others might be full-time work for a few weeks: creating the fall catalog and mailing it out or

3

building a new web site. Some projects take just a few hours: finding a new supplier to replace the one that is unreliable or hiring staff for the summer rush. It is a good idea to think of our opportunities and problems as projects. If we can say, "Here's where I am now and here's where I want to be," then we've defined a project.

*P*roject management helps by bringing problems under control.

What Is Management?

Everyone talks about management, but nobody stops to explain what it is. What do we really mean when we talk about managing something? We can understand that best if we look at the opposite of management. In a business, if something isn't *under management,* then it's *out of control.*

When a situation is out of control, we don't know what's going on. We don't know how bad it is, we don't know what it's going to cost us, and we don't know what to do about it. Here are some common out-of-control situations I've seen in small businesses:

▶ The books are not up to date.

▶ You can't get the supplies or inventory you need.

▶ You aren't getting the word out—advertising isn't working.

▶ Your team isn't getting the job done, and you don't know why.

▶ You promised work to a customer and can't deliver on time.

Think: Are any of these happening in your business right now? Or is some other situation out of control? Whatever situation is out of control, that's a problem. It's a risk to your business. Bringing the situation under control and solving the problem is a project.

When a situation is out of control, we want to bring it under management. There are three basic steps to taking care of any project: prepare, do, and follow through. Let's look at these in a bit more detail.

Prepare

▶ *Investigation:* What's really going on?

▶ *Evaluation:* Is it worth fixing? How big is the problem?

▶ *Planning:* What do we want to do about it?

▶ *Getting ready:* Get the people and things you need.

Do

▶ *Action:* Doing the work and fixing the problem.

▶ *Tracking:* Making sure our work follows the plan and fixes the problem.

▶ *Control:* If tracking shows us that we're off track, taking action to keep things under control.

Follow Through

▶ *Delivery:* Finishing the project, delivering the results, and making sure everyone knows it's done.

▶ *Maintenance:* Keeping up the good results through production management—monitoring, control, and improvement.

Whether we're bringing a situation under control, solving a problem, or making a dream come true, those three steps—*prepare, do, follow through*—are the essence of project management. In three steps, we *get it done right!*

A project in three steps: prepare, do, follow through.

Preventing a problem through preparation costs one-tenth what it will take to fix the problem if you let it happen.

Project Management Is Good Medicine

A project fixes your business the way a good trip to the doctor heals your body. Let's say that you like to walk or run, but you sprain your ankle. Here's the doctor's "prepare, do, follow through" plan for you:

▶ *Diagnosis and preparation.* He takes an X-ray to find out if the ankle is just sprained or it's broken. Good news—it's just a sprain. Now he can fix the right problem. He prepares a treatment with a bandage and a prescription.

▶ *Do.* He bandages the ankle. You learn to use a crutch for two weeks and he tells you when to apply heat and cold. He sees you each week to make sure the swelling is going down. If it's not, then he'll do a new diagnosis—maybe an MRI—to find out what is wrong.

▶ *Follow through.* After two weeks, you're up and walking. You see a physical therapist to work out an exercise schedule that will get you back to your full routine without risk of re-injury. You follow it and you're back in production—doing your exercise and staying healthy.

The Lesson: Good project managers think like doctors. They identify the problem before they run around trying to fix things.

Prepare: Investigate, Evaluate, Plan, and Get Ready

Preparation is the most important part of managing a project. If we don't prepare well, either the project will fail or it will take ten times longer than it should. Imagine going on vacation without preparing: you forget things you wanted to bring, you run out of gas on the road, and you get lost. All of these would be easy to prevent with preparation: a packing list, a trip to the gas station, and a map. Preparation is easy. Doing work without being prepared is a hassle and costs a lot.

Let's drop our opinions and deal with what's real.

Investigation means getting the facts before we decide what to do. Too often, we are too quick to say, "The vendor is the problem, let's get a new vendor," or "Fire the guy and get someone else to do the job," or "There's no way to fix this, we just have to live with it." Instead, let's get real. Let's gather the facts and understand the situation.

Evaluation means *fact-based decision making*. It means deciding to do what is best for the business, instead of flying off the handle and reacting. We look at the facts and answer three questions:

- ▶ *Feasibility.* Can we fix this problem? Most problems have a solution, but a few do not.
- ▶ *Value.* Is it worth fixing? If there's a dent in our truck, it may be cheaper to live with the dent than get it fixed. But if the truck won't run, we need to fix the truck or get a new one.
- ▶ *Basic approach.* How are we going to handle this problem? We decide what we need to do—fix or replace? And we decide who will do it—do we do it ourselves, call on our team, or get someone from the outside? If we're not sure yet, then we do some more investigation to figure out the best approach to the problem.

We *plan* by coming up with a detailed, step-by-step recipe for what we are going to do, just like when we're cooking.

- ▶ We list our resources, the ingredients.
- ▶ We pick our team, the cooks.
- ▶ We list each step of work, the recipe.
- ▶ We describe the end result.

In project management, everything gets written down. We need a writ-

Project Management on the Movie Set

One industry that does good project management in almost everything it does is the movie and television business. Whether it's a TV commercial or a Hollywood blockbuster, there's always a script and everyone goes over it with care. Before the cameras roll, there's a walk-through. Everyone knows exactly what he or she will be doing. Why are moviemakers so careful? There are two reasons. First, it saves time and money. A film session works only if the direction, the sound, the action, and the lighting are all right. One mistake ruins the shoot—and that costs lots of money. (We're talking thousands of dollars an hour, even for a simple commercial.) The other reason is safety. Scenes involving stunts like crashing cars and falling people require very careful walk-throughs.

The Lesson: Learn from the best. Prepare together and the team will succeed.

ten plan to bring things under control. When I'm doing a small project that will take me only two hours, I spend half an hour writing the plan. That prevents the project from becoming a four-hour hassle.

When we've defined the problem or opportunity and then come up with a plan for a solution, there's one more step of preparation. We ask: Do we have everything we need? Does each person know how to do his or her job? If so, we're ready to go. If not, then we get ready—we get the right people, we buy the supplies, we walk through the plan and make sure everyone knows his or her part.

When you have everything you need and everyone understands his or her part in the plan, you're ready for action.

Do: Action, Tracking, and Control

Now, the team gets moving. Each step of the plan is executed. The work gets done. And while it is getting done, you—the project manager—make sure it gets done. We make sure each person has what he or she needs to start working, we check that nobody gets stuck, and we check each job when it is done. If every small step is done right, then the whole project will come in on time, within budget, and with high quality. That's what it means to *get it done right!*

Even when we are doing the work ourselves on a one-person project, we should still keep track of our work and check off the steps as we go. Cooks make sure every ingredient goes into the cake; we should do our work with the same care.

7

We can understand the idea of *control* by thinking about a car trip. To get safely to the right destination, we need to control our driving in these six ways:

▶ *Stay on the road.* We keep an eye out while we're driving. If we start to drift out of lane, we correct our course. Similarly, if the task isn't getting done right, we stop, adjust, and do it right.

▶ *Eliminate repeating distractions.* If the reason we drifted out of lane is that our pet cat is jumping around the car, we stop the car and put the cat in a carrier before we have an accident. Similarly, if we keep getting interrupted or our tools aren't working or someone isn't showing up on the job, we take care of this problem before it derails the project.

▶ *Keep up to speed.* We want to arrive on time. So we make sure that we reach each milestone—each stop along the way—on time. If we're running behind, we take fewer breaks or speed up our driving. If we can't do that, we have to adjust our schedule.

▶ *Follow the route.* We make sure not to get lost when we're driving. On a project, our plan is like a road map. We make sure we follow all the steps in the right order.

▶ *Deal with roadblocks.* We might come upon road construction and be told to take a detour. In that case, we need to come up with a mini-plan, a small project to deal with the roadblock. We want to make sure we don't get lost and we want to adjust our route and our schedule to get to our destination in the best way that we can. On a project, if we lose a worker, some supply doesn't arrive, or a technique doesn't work, we need to replan and readjust.

▶ *Handle any really big problems.* Once in a while, things go so wrong that we need to revise our plan altogether. Say the car breaks down on the way to an important out-of-town meeting. Maybe it's time to rent a car or head for the airport—or reschedule the meeting.

As you can see, there are various levels of control, from very low to very high. Some take seconds; others might take hours. To succeed, we need to do all of them. It's not as hard as you might think. Here's what they all have in common:

- *Pay attention.*
- *Decide what to do.*
- *Take action fast.*
- *Make sure you're back on course.*

There is a method for this called *Plan, Do, Check, Act (PDCA)*, which we will discuss in Chapter 16, Quality: Eliminate Error.

When we pay attention to what's going on and make the right response—not too big and too small—we roll rapidly in the right direction. We keep doing that until all the steps are done and we're ready to follow through.

Follow Through: Delivery and Maintenance

When all the work is done, the project isn't really complete yet. Exactly what we need to do will vary from one project to the next. Here's a checklist; do any of these that you need to do on each project.

- *Deliver the result.* Physically send the product to the customer and make sure he or she gets it.
- *Install the product.* Some items require physical assembly or installation. Either we do this or we make sure that the customer does and that he or she has it working right.
- *Test end to end* to make sure everything is working right.
- *Provide training or instructions*, including training for new people who might come later, after the customer is using the product. We must make sure that this training lets the customer use the product and get benefits. It can't be just off-the-shelf training that says, "Here's how it works and what to do." Training must be focused on real benefits to your business or the customer.
- *Plan for operation and maintenance*, also called *production support*. Who will grease the wheels every year? Who does the customer call when the thing breaks?
- *Ensure customer delight.* Check with the customer to make sure that he or she has everything needed and expected and is delighted with you and your company. If not, make it right before it's too late.
- *Close the contract.* Get paid and make sure all your vendors get paid and all contracts are signed off.

When you have done all of these, you have a completed project and a delighted customer.

Internal and External Projects

External proj-ects make you money. Internal projects get your business running right.

Some projects are internal. They don't make money directly, but they change the way you work. Maybe you install a new bookkeeping system or you launch a new advertising campaign. For these projects, your customer is inside the company. In fact, your customer may be you! Still, you want to do them well. When an internal project is complete, then you should have a newer, easier way of working. It should help you do a better job and be more efficient. You should see less hassle and a bigger bottom line.

External projects are projects for customers. When we succeed on an external project, we make money and delight the customer. There are several great things about delighted customers:

▶ *Delighted customers come back for more.* That's how we get repeat business.

▶ *Delighted customers refer their friends and colleagues.* That's how our business grows.

▶ *Delighted customers provide references and give us examples for case studies.* That's how we show new customers what we do, speeding up our sales cycle to get more new business.

▶ *Delighting customers is what small business is all about.* Sure, we want to make money. But if that were all there was to it, we probably wouldn't run our own business. In small business, we and our teams get joy from a job well done, from helping a customer solve a problem. We succeed by helping others.

Conclusion: Project Management for Your Business

In the next 21 chapters, you'll learn all you need to know to make projects work. I hope that you'll make this book a workbook. Maybe you're already working on a project or you know what opportunity or problem you want to start with. If so, dive in. If not, take some time to think about which project matters most to your business. Is there one big roadblock in your way?

Is there something that keeps going wrong, over and over? Or is there a big opportunity—a chance to grow or change your business? If you've taken some time to think about that, read Chapter 2, Small Business Projects, for some ideas. You can also go out to the web site for this book, www.qualitytechnology.com/DoneRight, and pick up a survey to help you figure out what your next project should be, along with plenty of other templates and tools.

Chapter 2

Small Business Projects

WHEN BIG COMPANIES THINK ABOUT PROJECTS, THEY ARE USU-
ally talking about teams of ten or 50 or over a hundred
working for months or years. In small businesses, we are
talking of teams of one, or three, or five and a project
might get done in a week. Even so, I think project management is even more important for small companies than for big ones. A big
company can afford to blow a few million dollars and just write it off. For
example, one large state identified over 25 projects in trouble that were an
average of over $4 million over budget. That's $100 million down the tubes!
I can't afford to waste $1,000. And I bet you're in the same boat.

So, project management is about success for your business. In this chapter, you'll learn:

- ▶ where external and internal projects fit into your business
- ▶ the eight ways projects benefit a business
- ▶ who's who on a project
- ▶ and the 14 questions to ask on every project

Where Do Projects Fit into Your Business?

Small businesses need project success—we simply can't afford to waste money the way big companies do.

In Chapter 1, Get It Done Right! we talked about external projects for your customers and internal projects to improve your business. Figure 2-1 will help you figure out which type of projects you do at your company.

Some companies focus on external projects—they do unique, custom work for their customers, and the customers pay when they *get it done right!* In Figure 2-1, I call these Type 1 companies. Other companies, such as manufacturers, wholesalers, and retailers, make money by making or selling products or buying and selling products. In Figure 2-1, these are called Type 2 companies. Both types of companies benefit from projects and from good project management, but in different ways.

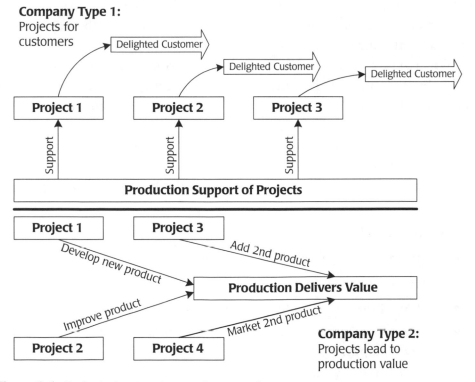

Figure 2-1. Projects for two types of companies

External Projects: Making Money from Projects

Type 1 companies do external projects. Their customers pay for them to finish projects and deliver results. Here are some examples:

- *A law firm* that handles cases for clients

- *A catering company* that supplies food and beverages for weddings and parties

- *A web design company* that might make a web site for your business

- *An architect and a construction company* that do renovations or build buildings for people or for other companies

- *A production company* that makes TV commercials

Type 1 companies may work for consumers or for other businesses. They may offer products, services, or solutions. They might be in manufacturing or be more white-collar. What all Type 1 companies have in common is that every job they do is unique. So each job must be done differently. That makes it a project. Type 1 companies generally have fewer clients than Type 2 companies and each client pays more money, because the company is doing specialized, custom work.

Listen to your customers. They'll tell you what you need to improve. Then put a deadline on that improvement and make it a project.

When Type 1 companies do good work on projects, they deliver on time, within budget, and give the customers everything they wanted and more. As a result, when the customers pay their bills, the company makes good money—lots of money for relatively little work. The company doesn't lose money running around fixing things after the fact. And satisfied customers come back and bring their friends.

When a Type 1 company doesn't do a good job at project management, here's what happens:

- Projects get done late.

- Customers don't get what they want or expect.

- What customers get doesn't work right and they are not satisfied.

- On fixed-price projects, the company loses money.

- On projects where the customer pays for the time spent, the customer is very unhappy.

- There is a lot of conflict.

- The customer won't always pay the full bill.

- The customer doesn't come back and probably tells his or her friends not to work with the company, either.

As you can see, good project management is essential to a Type 1 com-

Do Your Projects Make Money?

If you do projects for customers, you already know some project management. Evaluate your ability and results with these questions:

- ▶ Do your projects get done on time?
- ▶ Do you make money on most projects?
- ▶ Do your customers ever say, "This isn't what I wanted?" Or is it easy to get thanks and referrals?
- ▶ Do you keep track of work as it gets done? Do you keep track of time and money spent as you go along, or do you just figure it out afterwards?
- ▶ Does your team have all the skills, tools, and support to get the job done right?

Don't judge yourself, but do identify your strengths and weaknesses. Then, as you read *Project Management for Small Business Made Easy,* focus on getting better in the areas that most need improvement.

The Lesson: In work, everything connects like a chain. Honest assessment lets us find the weakest link, so we can make it stronger.

pany—projects are linked directly to customer satisfaction and profit.

Internal Projects: Working Smarter

Type 2 companies, on the other hand, make money by selling many of the same product or service to customers. Here are some examples:

- ▶ A *beauty parlor* that sees many customers each day
- ▶ A *restaurant or store* that buys things from manufacturers and sells to customers
- ▶ A *manufacturing company* that makes something and sells it
- ▶ A *building supply or auto parts company* that sells equipment, parts, and materials to other companies
- ▶ A *video store* that rents and sells movies to customers

Since Type 2 companies don't make money doing projects, it might seem that project management is less important for these companies. But that is not true. Projects simply have a different role in Type 2 companies. Instead of making money directly, projects in Type 2 companies help the company solve problems and work smarter, so they can stay in business and make more money.

Type 2 companies do projects for four reasons:

An internal project is an investment that pays off by making the business better.

15

▶ *To realize new opportunities or dreams.* For example, you might launch a new product or open a new location.

▶ *To do occasional work.* If you put out a new catalog once each season or once a year or if you do an annual inventory or run a closeout sale, that's a project.

▶ *To solve problems.* If your assembly line is breaking down, or you can't hire good workers fast enough, or something else is wrong, you can launch a project to define the problem and solve it.

▶ *To work smarter.* Here, we're talking about effectiveness and efficiency. Effectiveness is about doing a better job. Efficiency is about doing the same job, only faster or at lower cost. Working smarter is important because, if you don't work smarter, your competitors will. And when they do, they'll have a better product, or better customer service, or lower prices. Then you'll lose market share.

One way to work smarter is to use new technology. We might get a computer network or install a computer program that is designed to run our business. We might buy more fuel-efficient trucks or better equipment. But better technology only gives us the opportunity to work smarter and save money. Internal projects need to make sure that, when we're done installing the new technology, we're actually working in new ways, and that those new ways of working actually are more effective and more efficient. Otherwise, the new technology is just a waste of time and money.

More or Less Unique

Projects You Already Do

Make a list of projects that you already do. If you run a Type 2 company, what things come up occasionally, such as creating catalogs, running marketing campaigns or sales, doing inventory, cleaning shop, renegotiating contracts, and planning your next quarter or next year? Each of these is a project. Make a list of occasional or scheduled projects and make a list of projects you are working on now.

The Lesson: We're all doing projects all the time. Once we realize it, we can do each one better.

Although I talked about two distinct types of businesses above, there can be a range between the two. Let's take a look at one industry—home repair and improvement—and see all the possibilities. We'll start with the pure Type 2 company—all routine work—and move up to the pure Type 1 company that makes its living doing projects for clients.

- A store like Home Depot or a hardware store does no projects for customers at all.
- A plumbing repair service like Roto-Rooter that unclogs and fixes pipes can look at its work as routine or can see each job as a small project.
- An electrician who does contract work—general repair and also installation of new wiring—does some routine work and some projects.
- A general contractor who does some routine work, some renovation, and some building of new homes, is doing some of the work as routine, but some large projects.
- A custom architectural firm that designs and implements major renovations and builds custom homes is doing all the money-making work as projects.

As you can see, there is a range in the amount of project work we might do for customers and also in the size and diversity of projects. Two other factors come into play when we look at how to use project management in our small businesses:

- *Some companies are hybrids, doing some routine work and some project work.* A common example is a restaurant—a Type 2 business—that also has a catering service for special events—a Type 1 business.
- *Some industries change faster than others.* If you do plumbing repair, you're probably doing it pretty much the same way that your father did—except that some pipes are now plastic. But if you do computer repair, your equipment changes several times a year.

When we put all this together—when we see if we make money by projects, how big our projects are, and how fast our industry changes—we can decide what types of projects will help our company grow.

Do You Have Money to Burn?

Do you have money to burn? Of course not—no small business owner does. That's why businesses need good project management. But that leads to another question as well—how much money do you have for projects and on learning better project management?

The key question here is how much money you have for projects. That varies a lot depending on the type of business you're in. How much money and work time do you have left over after you pay for the essentials every month? If you take your gross revenue (all the money you take in from sales) minus the cost of goods sold (all the money you spend buying things to sell), then minus the cost of overhead (rent and other regular bills), that's the amount of money you have to play with. Some businesses—such as consulting firms—have a lot of money left over. They charge high prices, but don't need to buy anything. Others, like grocery stores, have to buy a lot of products, sell them at competitive prices, and then throw away what doesn't sell. They have very little money left over.

That money is money you can put in your pocket or use for projects. But if the projects will increase your revenue or decrease your costs in the future, then the project will pay off.

Sometimes, we have to do a project and we can't afford it with money on hand. Then we might have to take out a loan or borrow on a line of credit. Or maybe we can do the project slowly, a bit at a time, using our own time or our team.

Eight Ways Projects Benefit Your Business

What makes for better business? Ultimately, there is only one measure—net revenue, which is your gross revenue (total income) minus your costs (total expenses). This one measure can be broken down into three basic categories:

▶ *Increase gross revenue.* If we can sell more—by increasing our price, by selling more of what we already sell, or by selling new products *without increasing our cost per sale,* that increases net revenue.

▶ *Reduce costs.* If we can do the same amount of sales at lower cost, that increases net revenue.

▶ *Reduce risks.* There are risks—things that might happen—associated with any business. For instance, as a business, we have personal information about our employees and credit card information about our customers. If this information is stolen from us and misused, it can cost us a lot. Recently, a computer hacker broke into a Texas university and stole over 37,000 people's credit card information. It cost the university over $170,000 in lost computer time and work to warn people of the theft. If we make our systems more secure or simply buy the right type of insurance, we can bring these risks under management.

We can break these three general ways to improve our business into eight

Which Type of Business Are You In?

So, review what you've read above and answer these questions:

▶ Which type of business are you in: Type 1, Type 2, or a hybrid, a business with two different parts?

▶ If you do projects for customers, how large are they? How much do you get paid for each one—what's the range from smallest to largest? How long do they take?

▶ How fast does your industry's technology change? How often do you need to get new tools and learn to use them?

Write down your answers and you'll be ready to pick a project and grow your business.

specific ways a project can help. Each project we do is worth doing because it does one or more of these eight things:

▶ *Brings a new product or service to market* so we have something new to sell.

▶ *Increases production* so we can make more things to sell. (This helps only if we have customers who will buy those things.)

▶ *Increases market share,* for example, through a new advertising campaign or better marketing.

▶ *Reaches new markets or customers,* for example, by opening a new location or starting to sell through a web site.

▶ *Markets or delivers* to our customers in new ways, increasing sales or lowering the cost of sales.

▶ *Speeds up cycle time,* getting products to market faster, completing jobs faster, getting supplies faster, and making decisions faster, which makes us more flexible and competitive.

▶ *Reduces or avoids costs,* changing the way we get supplies or the way we work to reduce waste and cost and increase net revenue.

▶ *Reduces risk and protects assets,* to improve protection of our tangible assets—preventing damage, fraud, and theft—and our intangible assets—things like customer good will, employee loyalty, and recognition of ourselves and our company as reliable professionals and good citizens.

When someone suggests a project, we should always ask, "Why should I do this? Why is it good for my business?" Our answer should be phrased in terms of one or more of the eight benefits listed above. If we can, we should assign a number, called the *hard-dollar value.*

For example, we might be able to say, "Our supply contract for widgets is coming up for renewal. If we open the bidding up to multiple vendors, we believe we can get high-quality widgets for ten cents less than we do now. We sell 12,000 widgets per month. If we save ten cents per widget and keep our price the same, net revenue should increase by $1,200 per month, or $14,400 per year. Or, we could reduce the price of our widgets by five cents and sell 15,000 per month. We currently make $1.00 net revenue per widget. By lowering our cost and increasing sales, instead of making $12,000 net revenue per month on widgets, we would make $15,750 per month, an increase of $3,750 per month, or $45,000 per year."

The value of an internal project is in how it changes the way we do business.

A clear statement like that gives us a very good reason to do the project. Since renegotiating the contract will cost a lot less than $14,400 and way less than $45,000, it is certainly worth doing. We can make a clear statement of hard-dollar value if we think about how this change *will change the way we do business.*

Sometimes, we can't predict exactly how much benefit we will gain from a project, but at least we can describe the type of benefit we will get. This is one way of defining *soft-dollar value.*

Here is one example: "Customers complain that we do not have certain popular products in stock, and we lose the chance to sell them. We have identified these products. (See attached list.) If we work with current and new suppliers to keep these items in stock, we will sell more of them and make more money. We will also keep customers who now go to competing stores to get what they need when we don't have it and sometimes never come back to our store."

Sometimes, we can make a statement that describes both hard-dollar value and soft-dollar value. Here is another version of that last example, from a company that has a bit more data. "We have tracked how often popular products are missing from our shelves. The attached list shows our ten most popular products that are not always in stock, how many days we were out of stock last month, and how much of each we usually sell per day. Based on this chart, monthly gross revenue would increase by $12,800 if these products were in stock all the time. In addition, by keeping these products in stock, we will retain customers who are now going to other stores to get their favorite brands and sometimes not coming back."

Before you launch a project, ask, "Why is this good for my business?" Then write up a statement that includes hard-dollar value, soft-dollar value, or both.

Who's Who on a Project

Every project has people in several different roles. The central person is the project manager. He or she plans the project, pulls the team together, communicates with everyone, and makes sure that the job gets done right. Part of the project manager's job is to explain to everyone else what his or her role on the project is and how it is crucial to project success. The project manager must communicate with everyone and persuade each person to do his or her part. Table 2-1: Who's Who on a Project shows the roles and how the project manager works with each one.

Whether a project is a one-person job or involves lots of people, the key is to know who needs to do what and when and to make sure that they do it.

Remember that a role is not the same thing as a person. In fact, on a small project, you might be the customer, the executive manager, the sponsor, and the team! For example, suppose you decide that you need a new piece of bookkeeping software for your three-person company where you do all the bookkeeping. You might do some research, decide what to buy, and purchase and install it yourself. As owner of the company, you decided the project was worth doing; that makes you the sponsor. As executive manager, you'll decide when to do the project and when to get other work done. You'll be doing the work with the new software; that makes you the cus-

Stakeholder	Role	How Project Manager (PM) Works with Stakeholder
Sponsor	Kicks off the project and provides the money	PM provides regular status reports and reports special problems. Also makes requests for additional funds if needed.
Executive Managers	Run the company that is doing the project	PM provides regular status reports and reports special problems. Also goes to them if there are irresolvable problems getting people to work on the project or if there is a conflict between the project and company operations or policy.
Customers	Receive primary benefit from project results	PM elicits their requirements during planning. PM manages their expectations and documents changes to the specifications at their request. PM makes sure that they are satisfied with project results at each gate and works with them to define necessary changes to the project or product.
Project Manager		PM is responsible for running the project with the team on a daily basis.
Project Team	Works full time or the most time on the project, planning and doing the actual work to create the result	PM leads team members to work together to achieve project goals with high quality on time and under budget. PM meets with them daily or weekly to update project status and address any possible problems or changes to the plan.
Vendor	Provides products or services to the project team	PM defines project needs, negotiates purchase agreements or contracts or has the team do this, and approves the activities.
Peripheral stakeholder	Has some occasional contact with part of the product	PM identifies and makes sure that the project plan includes their requirements. PM ensures that they test and approve any components they will use.
Other Stakeholder	Anyone else connected to the project	PM identifies additional stakeholders and communicates with them as needed for project success.

Table 2-1. Who's who on a project

tomer. You figured out what you wanted, bought it, and got it running; that makes you the project manager and the team.

For each project, go through Table 2-1 and decide if that role applies to the project. If it does, name the person, explain the role to him or her, and work with him or her—using tools from this book—to define exactly what work is to be done, schedule it, and *get it done right!*

The 14 Questions for Every Project

Planning is really simple. All we have to do is ask the right questions and then write down our answers. Here are the 14 crucial questions to ask in planning any project. After each question except the last, you'll see a term in italics that defines the area of project management knowledge related to the question.

*M*ake your plans clear and complete.

1. *Why* are we doing this project? Why is it good for our company? Focus on value, benefit, and purpose. *Project scope management.*
2. *What* are we making? Define the *scope* of the project. *Project scope management.*
3. *How* will we make it? *Project scope management.*
4. *When* will we do it? *Project time management.*
5. *How much* time will it take? *Project time management.*
6. *How much* money will it cost? *Project cost management.*
7. *What makes it good? Project quality management.*
8. *How can we make sure* it gets done? *Project risk management.*
9. *What could go wrong? Project risk management.*
10. *Who* will do it? *Project human resources management.*
11. *How will we keep in touch and stay on the same page? Project communications management.*
12. *What do we need? How will we get it? Project procurement management.*
13. *How do we keep it all together? What do we do* if things change in the middle? *Project integration management.*
14. W*hether* we should do the project or cancel it? If things go wrong during a project, we can say, "No, we should cancel this project." We should always keep in mind the possibility of cancellation. If we know the project could be canceled, we'll be sure to get it done right.

The areas of project management knowledge are defined by the *Project Management Institute (PMI),* the global professional association that certifies project managers and helps the field keep growing. It has over 200,000 members worldwide. We'll talk more about the project management areas of knowledge in the next chapter.

Conclusion: Pick a Project and Go!

Outside of NASA (the U.S. space agency, where a lot of project management ideas were first developed), project management isn't rocket science. It's mostly common sense. Aphorisms like "measure twice, cut once," "a stitch in time saves nine," and "anything worth doing is worth doing right" explain what makes project management essential to our businesses. The ideas are straightforward.

The challenge is not to our brains, but to our will. Are we willing to change our habits? It is said that one definition of insanity is to keep doing things the same way and expect different results. If you're holding this book in your hands, you must want something to work better. Are you willing to change the way that you work?

If so, I'd like you to do more than read *Project Management for Small Business Made Easy*. I'd like you to *use* it. To do that, you need a project. Here are four possibilities:

▶ *Take a project you are doing right now* and apply what you learn as you go.

▶ *Start a small project that's good for your company.* After reading these two chapters, you may have realized what your next opportunity or most urgent problem is. If so, go for it! Make that your project. But make sure that you don't bite off more than you can chew—there's a lot still to learn!

▶ *Pick a project for learning.* If you're under a lot of pressure at work, pick something else—a volunteer project or something at home. Pick something small and fun. A friend of mine learned project management from one of my books while designing a web site for a not-for-profit association. I do one project for learning each year; one year, I set up a home entertainment center.

▶ *Make learning project management your project.* If you're really busy, then you can simply make a project out of learning project management. Get a notebook and write down two or three things you can do differently each time you finish reading a chapter. Then put your ideas into practice!

Learning is easier with tools and forms. Be sure to check out www.qualitytechnology.com/DoneRight for the tools that work with this book. And read on to learn about stages and gates and the project management knowledge areas in Chapter 3, Prepare, Do, Follow Through.

Chapter 3

Prepare, Do, Follow Through

IN A SMALL BUSINESS, WE'RE SO BUSY THAT WE OFTEN SKIP OR SKIMP ON PLAN-ning. We think, "I've just got to get this done" or "I know how to do this." Then we dive in, get to work, and find ourselves running around with work that's full of hassles. And we have no idea how costly those hassles are, but they actually eat up all of our profit. We lose money. Our work is no fun, either.

When projects take longer than expected, they waste time and money. Worse, nearly half of all projects fail altogether. That's a huge loss—one that small businesses can't afford.

The goals of project management are simple: make sure we succeed and don't waste time and money.

Big businesses have taken the time to figure out how much planning pays off. The numbers are pretty astounding. In every industry, each dollar spent on planning and preparation saves $10 on project work or $100 on fixing problems after the project is done. This is called the *1:10:100 rule*: it shows the ratio of time or money across preparing, doing, and following through. That's right. A well-planned project will take one tenth as much time as the same project done with no planning at all. And every hour of planning saves ten hours of project time or 100 hours of hassle later on.

In this chapter, you will learn:

▶ Why careful preparation and good project work are essential to your business

▶ How to make sure you have a good plan before you get to work with stages and gates

▶ The nine areas of project management: everything you need to plan and manage a project

To put it simply, when we just jump in and get to work, we're being sloppy. That costs us a lot more than we think it does. *Project Management for Small Business Made Easy* takes the best practices of project management from companies that can't afford to make mistakes and teaches them to you. In some industries—like aerospace and medicine—life is on the line. In others—like Hollywood—time costs thousands of dollars a minute. Using what they know in our own small businesses makes the difference between losing money and making a good living, between burnout and enjoying our work, between shutting down and succeeding.

Businesses, Projects, and Systems

If you dent your fender, your car will still run. But if anything goes wrong with the power system—the carburetor, the fuel line, the engine, the drive shaft, the gears and axles, the wheels—the car isn't going to go anywhere. That's because your car is a system. There are some fundamental rules of systems:

▶ When one part of a system breaks down, the whole system doesn't work.

▶ If we change one part of a system, we change the way the whole system works.

▶ When the parts of a system don't communicate or don't work together well, the system fails.

▶ When a system has problems, the symptoms are in one place, but the source of the problem is likely to be somewhere else.

▶ When things around a system change, the system has to change to adapt and keep working.

Your business is like a car: if one part breaks down, the whole thing won't go.

Just like a car's drive train, a small business is a system. And a project is a system, too. The most common complaint of a small business owner might be "I did almost everything right! How come it didn't work?" If you do body work on a car, getting almost everything right is good enough. But if you work on the engine, the fuel line, the steering, or the brakes, "almost" doesn't cut it. In small business—and on our projects—we have to plan everything and take care of all of the details.

There's a plus side to all of this. When we plan and prepare carefully, our work sings. It sails along smoothly. We're in the zone and we get even better results than we ever dreamed.

Stages and Gates

Make sure you're ready before you go.

Because of the 1:10:100 rule, it makes sense to break every project up into three stages. In Chapter 1, Get It Done Right!, we introduced those stages: prepare, do, and follow through.

Now, let's take a look at some difficult questions. How do you know when you're done preparing and you're ready to go? How much planning is enough? How much planning is too much?

On each project, we can answer those questions by putting a gate after each stage. A gate is a time we set aside to review the work we've done so far. And we pass through the gate and on to the next stage only if we've done good work and we're ready to go.

We put a preparation review gate at the end of preparation. We ask:

▶ *Was our investigation good?* Do we understand the problem correctly and clearly? Do we understand it well enough to fix it?

▶ *Was our evaluation good?* Is this opportunity worth the effort or is this problem worth fixing? Does the size of the project match the size of the problem?

▶ *Is our plan good?* A good plan covers all nine of the areas of project management that we'll discuss later in this chapter.

▶ *Are we ready?* Do we have everyone we need? Does everyone understand the problem and the project? Does everyone have the right skills? Do we have all the tools and materials we need to start the job? Is anything missing?

Are You Ready for the Long Ride?

There is a special kind of horse racing, called *endurance riding*, that gives us a model for how gate reviews should work. Horse and rider go for 50 miles or more with little rest. At the end of every stage of the race, a few times a day, there is a checkpoint or gate. You win by finishing the race first, but, if your horse is in no shape to ride, then you're out of the race. So you have to ride well and ride fast, but also take good care of your horse.

It's just the same on a project. We have to prepare well and do all our planning and all our work thoroughly. But we can't burn out or let our team burn out. At each gate, we review the work we've done. If it's not finished, we take time for rework. We also make sure that our team and we are ready for the next stage.

The Lesson: Break a project into stages and gates, take the gate reviews seriously, and you'll make the long haul.

The review process is real, not rote. As you ask each of these questions, fix anything that is unclear or incomplete, if it can be fixed quickly. Otherwise:

▸ Make notes to rework anything that needs more time.

▸ If there isn't too much rework, schedule a brief review of the changes.

▸ If there's a lot of rework, do it all and then hold a whole second review.

▸ Be ready and willing to cancel the project if you can't get the plan right or if the project just isn't worth doing.

When to Cancel a Project

*D*on't throw good money after bad.

Not every bright idea is a good idea. Not every good idea is worth doing. Not every idea that is worth doing can or should be done right now. As you plan, and especially at the preparation review gate, you should consider canceling the project. Why? Because it makes no sense to throw good money after bad. If a project can't be done, the sooner you stop it, the sooner you quit wasting precious time and money.

It's hard to give up on a plan. It hurts the ego. But, ultimately, we have to choose between our egos and our business. If we are humble enough to admit that our idea is bad or that we are overwhelmed and don't have what it takes to do a project right now, then we can stop the project and use our time and money well. If not, we're headed for humiliation, for failure, and for bigger problems with our company. We're a lot better off deciding what's good for our business than we are just plowing ahead trying to make a bad idea work.

When we review a project, we should go ahead only if we are confident of success. If we see problems we can't solve, it's time to stop or at least pause. When we pause, our next step depends on the size of the problem:

▶ *For a small problem,* get some expert help or do some brainstorming and think outside the box. If you can come up with a solution, add it to your plan and roll through the preparation gate.

▶ *For a medium-sized problem,* ask what you need to fix the problem. Sometimes, waiting is enough. Maybe you and your team are just too busy to do this right now. Maybe you need to hire someone with the right skills. Maybe you need to do another project first—like catching up on last year's bookkeeping and taxes before you plan next year's budget. Plan a way to get from where you are to a point where you can make this project work.

▶ *For a big problem,* be ready to cancel the project, before the project cancels your business.

Perparation is the most important part of any project, so we'll discuss the preparation stage in Chapters 4 through 12. If we pass through the preparation review gate, we start doing the work and tracking our progress. We'll discuss that in detail in Chapters 13 through 18. When we've done all the work in our plan, we're almost finished with the project. But there are three more steps: the doing gate, the follow-through stage, and the follow-through gate.

The doing gate is where we check that we did everything and that everything works. We make sure our product and we are fully ready for the customer. In follow-through, we deliver the project results to the customer: we handle delivery, installation, and training. In the follow-through gate, we ensure project completion and customer delight.

So far, we've looked at a project from beginning to end. We've looked at the stages and gates of project management in time. Now, we're going to shift our perspective. We're going to look across a project—what are all the things we need to manage? Those are defined in the nine areas of project management.

The Nine Areas of Project Management

Over the last 35 years, the Project Management Institute (PMI) has worked to define the field of project management as an independent profession and certify professionals in the field. You can learn more about it them at www.pmi.org. They offer this formal definition of a project: "a temporary endeavor undertaken to create a unique product, service, or result." Over the years, the PMI has discovered that there are nine areas we need to manage to make a project succeed. It calls these the "nine areas of project management knowledge." In terms of studying for certification, they are areas of knowledge. In terms of project success, they are areas of planning and work. We need to plan for and work in each of these nine areas as we prepare, do, and follow through on each project. Don't worry if this introduction to the nine areas is very short. They are covered in depth—and applied specifically to small businesses—in Chapters 6 through 12.

Scope: What and How

Project scope definition answers the questions "What are we making?" and "How will we make it?" The goal is to define everything we need to do to complete everything included in the product or result and nothing extra. Once we've defined that, our goal is to keep scope under control. We track our work and correct our course so that we do everything we need to do, we

Clear definition of what we are doing sets us on the path to success.

Spiral to Success

I have taught over 2,000 students in hundreds of project management classes. In every class, I ask for stories of success and failure. I've found this universal fact: from the very beginning, a project that has a clear scope definition is headed for success. When we know what we're making, we get the right people together, and we plan for time, cost, quality, and other project success factors. Then the right people doing the right job get the work done right. We stay focused, stay on time, and deliver the right stuff.

On the other hand, every poorly defined project is headed in a downward spiral. When we aren't clear about what we're doing, we're not sure who is best for the job. No one knows exactly what he or she should be doing. New things are thrown in and plans are changed all the time. Work starts and stops, time and money are wasted, and the project is spiraling toward disaster.

The Lesson: Define a clear goal, in detail, and spiral toward success.

deliver everything we're supposed to deliver, and we don't do anything extra.

Scope creep is a danger to any project. We start simple and then we say, "But I could do this, too. And why don't I do that, as well?" All of a sudden, we're doing so many things that we can't finish on time, we've blown our budget, and we have nothing to show for our work. By defining our goal clearly up front and allowing changes to the plan only when they are truly essential, we prevent scope creep.

You'll learn more about project scope management in Chapters 6 and 14.

Time: Effort and Duration

At the end of project scope management, we know what work we will be doing. In time planning, we prepare *activity lists*—we decide who will do what and when. From this, we can plan project *effort*, the number of person-hours of work to be done, and project *duration*, how long the project will take from start to finish. Project time management also includes time estimation and schedule control to make sure we're getting work done on time.

Cost: Estimates, Budgets, and Tracking

Track time and money as you go or your tank will run dry.

Once we've figured out our schedule, we can estimate what the project will cost. We build a budget and then we track the time and money we spend each week. If we don't track it as we go along, our schedule and budget will go out of control. We will fall behind and not even know it. We keep on top of the project by looking at the work we've accomplished, the time we've spent, and the money we've spent.

Quality: Make It Good

Improve your processes to save time, save money, and deliver the best.

There are two aspects to quality management. One is in designing the product or service—the project results. We should ask more than "What are we making?" We should ask, "What will make it really good?" If we ask that in planning, we can often get better results—a greater improvement of net revenue—for the same project cost. For example, a smart, savvy advertising campaign is far more successful than a dull campaign that costs just as much. The second part of quality management is about working smarter. Here, we focus on the quality of our process—on how we do the work, manage the project, and manage business and customer value. By improving the quality of the project, we increase the chances of delivering really good results on time and under budget.

Risk: Make Sure We Get It Done

Once we have a good plan, we have to make sure we can follow the plan. What if a key worker leaves the company? What if some other urgent project interrupts our work? What if some technical solution doesn't work or a supply is not available?

"What if?" is the central question of project risk management. We realize that the future is always uncertain—we don't know what will happen. So, we think about what might happen and write it down. Then we prepare for each thing that might change our project plan or get in the way of success. Once we're ready for any contingency, we keep risk under control by tracking events weekly and handling things if they look like they are about to happen or when they do.

Be ready for the unexpected—and move fast when the stuff hits the fan.

Human Resources: The Project Team

For small businesses, project human resources means getting the right people on the team for the job and making sure they can do the work. For each person on each job, we ask if they understand the work, if they have the right skills, and if they have the time to do the work. Any time one of those questions gets "no" for an answer, we find a solution: we explain the job, we get training or bring in an expert, or we give project work the priority it needs to get the job done right.

Communications: Keep Everyone on Board

In Chapter 2, Small Business Projects, we introduced the idea of all the people in different roles on the project—executives, customers, team members, and stakeholders. Project communications begins by figuring out who all of those people are. Then we figure out what we need to hear from them and what they need to hear from us. We plan, manage, and execute effective communications to make sure the plan includes everyone's perspective, that everyone understands the plan, and that everyone is on the same page and up to date when changes hit the project.

Management means helping everyone do a good job.

Procurement: Getting What We Need

For most small business projects, procurement is making a good shopping list and then making sure we get the right thing and that it comes in on time. In some cases, we may do some hunting for best prices. Sometimes, we have to deal with vendor selection and contract management as well.

Integration: Keeping It All Together

The eight knowledge areas we've just described are all tied together in one system. Here's an example.

Let's say our best worker wins the lottery and quits his job. That's an HR problem. But now we need to put the project on hold until we get someone new. That affects the schedule. The new person has a higher salary and our budget goes up. During the delay, a crucial product component is dropped from the vendor's product line (a procurement problem), so we have to change what we're making (scope) and see how that affects quality. All of this, of course, requires good communications. If our new design doesn't satisfy the customer, there is a risk of project failure.

Our ninth area, project integration management, means that we keep track of what is going on in all the other areas and deal with any changes to the project promptly and fully. This is also called *integrated change management*.

Conclusion: Tying It All Together

Back in the 1960s, people thought that managing scope, time, and cost was enough to *get it done right!* We've learned it takes more than that. Scope, time, and cost—doing the right work on time and within budget—are results that depend on good process. We can break out the nine areas as follows:

▶ **Results: Scope, Time, and Cost.** Make the right thing and deliver it on time and within budget.

▶ **Focus on process: Quality and Risk.** Quality management is about improving processes to make it good and work smart, so that we do a better job at lower cost with less work. Risk management recognizes that the future is uncertain, so we take time to plan and prepare for the unexpected.

▶ **Do supporting processes: Human Resources, Communications, and Procurement.** Support the team, keep everyone in the loop, and get what you need.

▶ **Pull it all together: Integration.** Remember: a project is a system. Change one part and all the other parts change. So, when change happens—to requirements, to schedule or budget, or anywhere else—we need to assess the consequences, plot a new course, and steer for success.

In the next two chapters, we'll get very clear about defining projects that will bring success to your business. In Chapter 4, we'll look at dreams and opportunities. In Chapter 5, you'll see how to use project management to solve problems in your business.

Chapter 4

Dreams and Opportunities

I F YOU RUN A SMALL BUSINESS, YOU HAVE A CHANCE TO DO WHAT YOU WANT without anyone telling you that you can't do it. If you have a dream, you can try to make it real. If you see an opportunity to make more money, to grow your business, or to do something you've always wanted to do, you can shoot for it. There's no one to tell you, "Hey, you can't do that."

But you might not succeed. In fact, the odds are against you. It's really hard to make dreams real. It's really hard to jump at the right moment, do just the right thing, and come out on top. Sure, the magazines are full of stories of people who did it. But that's because the people who didn't do it don't get stories.

Using project management, you can make dreams real. Using project management, you can seize an opportunity and make the most of it. Chapter 4, Dreams and Opportunities, will show you how.

Rules for Making Dreams Real

We all dream of more than we can do in a lifetime. It is good that our dreams are larger than life and that we have many of them, because dreams expand life, giving it meaning and value. But that means it's hard to make dreams real. Project management teaches seven lessons about how to make dreams real. These lessons are based on unchanging principles, so you can't get around them. Either you can learn them from others and make your dreams real, or you can learn them the hard way, by making your own mistakes. Here are the lessons:

We can make our dreams real with quality— one at a time.

- Pick one dream at a time and commit to pursuing it.
- Get a clear picture of your dream.
- Desire it, want it, love it. Ask for what you need to make the dream real.
- Get very clear about what the dream is. Make sure it is good for everyone involved and let others make it better by making it their dream, too.
- Keep at it. Work, rest to renew yourself, and work again.
- Make change happen. When a dream becomes real, it means destroying what was reality to make room for what's new.
- Let the dream grow. It's not all under our control. Unexpected things— some challenging, some wonderful—will happen. And then it will be done.

Two Dreams Are Too Many to Pursue

I learned this lesson the hard way. I'd started my own business and it was doing very well. I had money, success, and business savvy. I wanted to help a friend launch her musical career and I thought I could do it. In fact, I could. But I couldn't keep my business going and get her business growing at the same time. I could have done one or the other, but not both. When I tried to do both, I got fried. I got exhausted, and then sick, and I lost one business, nearly lost the other, and ended up deeply in debt. I worked my way back to success, but it took a while.

The Lesson: Don't overextend yourself. Make only one dream real at a time. Go after one opportunity at a time. Make only one big change to your business at a time.

Defining Your Dream or Opportunity

In small business, a dream or an opportunity is a chance to make things better. In business, that's usually, but not always, a chance to make more money.

To make more money or get more customers or grow the business or whatever, we need to change what we are doing. Only if we change what we're doing can we seize the opportunity and get the better results.

Defining an opportunity means defining the new results and defining the new ways we are going to work to get them. This is all part of planning. After we define the opportunity and plan how to get there, we may decide that it isn't worth it. So we'll define the opportunity, plan how to get there, and then evaluate whether it's worth doing.

There are two steps to defining the opportunity. First, we look at what will be different from the way it is now. Then we look at how the business will work when it is making the dream come true or realizing the opportunity.

What's Different?

How will your business—and your life—be different when you realize your dreams?

So, the key to defining an opportunity is to ask, "What will be different?" Specifically, you want to write down the changes in the results and the process:

▶ *The results.* How will your business results be different once you've realized the opportunity? Will you make more money, gain new customers, have customers buying over the internet instead of by phone?

▶ *The process.* Describe the difference in *how* each person will work. Maybe you'll spend more time selling to customers while others work more in other areas. Or maybe you'll do work more in other areas while others spend time doing sales. Maybe you'll all do the same jobs, but on laptops and with cell phones, working from home and on the road, instead of coming into the office.

You can use Table 4-1 to describe and define an opportunity.

How Will It Work?

The best way to describe a new opportunity combines creativity with good analysis. To ensure creativity, write down your idea in one or two paragraphs before you use Table 4-1. Write it so that anyone in your company could understand it. Don't write more than a sentence about *why* you want to do it; that will come later. Then add good analysis to your creativity by filling out a copy of Table 4-1. You can get an editable copy of the tool at www.qualitytechnology.com/DoneRight.

Show what you've written to everyone whose job will change with the new

The Results of the Opportunity This section describes business results before and after the change.		
The Question	**How It Is Now** **(before any change)**	**How It Will Be After the** **Opportunity Is Realized**
Money		
Gross revenue/month		
Net revenue/month		
Customers		
Number of customers/night		
Type of customers		
Staff		
New staff		
People in different jobs		
Jobs that will be lost		
Products and Services		
New products or services		
Products or services that will be eliminated		
Changes or upgrades to products or services		
Tools and Equipment		
New tools and equipment		
Tools and equipment that will go away		
Tools and equipment that will be replaced or upgraded		
The New Way of Working This section describes our work process—how we do our work before and after the change.		
Executive leadership functions		
How will owners', executives', and senior managers' jobs change?		

Table 4-1. Opportunity definition tool (continued on next page)

The New Way of Working *(continued)* This section describes our work process—how we do our work before and after the change.		
The Question	**How It Is Now (before any change)**	**How It Will Be After the Opportunity Is Realized**
Product and Service Development		
What will change in the ways we create our products and deliver our services?		
Marketing		
What will change in the ways we market?		
Sales		
What will change in the ways we sell?		
Client Services and Customer Support		
What will change in the ways we service clients and respond to customer support requests?		
Financial Operations		
What will change in the ways we do accounting and financial work?		
Research and Analysis		
What will change in the ways we do research and analysis?		

Table 4-1. Opportunity definition tool (continued)

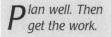

Plan well. Then get the work.

opportunity. Get their ideas and make it even better. In fact, make it as good as you can. Come up with a realistic, solid plan that makes your business better.

How much time should you spend defining an opportunity? That depends on four factors:

▶ *How big is the expected change in results?* The bigger the chance for growth, the more time it's worth exploring the idea.

▶ *How big is the change in the way you work?* Note that this can differ for different players.

▶ *How big is the risk?* If this opportunity is a real challenge—if it relies on things outside your control or if it may just be too big or too difficult—then plan it and evaluate it closely before you go ahead.

▶ *How much will it cost?* Time and money spent on planning should be proportional to the investment.

Put lots of planning, thinking, and research into a new opportunity—look before you leap. Why? Because every opportunity you invest in cuts off other opportunities. Moving your business into the future is like climbing a huge tree with many branches. Every time you step out on one branch, you leave all the other branches behind. You move ahead, but you limit your choices to the branches of this branch. It is very costly to go back to another branch and very risky to leap from one branch to another. So, before we set a new direction, we should be sure that the branch we choose will take us where we want to go.

To do this, you might want to prepare a full business plan or draft a brochure describing the business. Note, however, that business plans are usually for investors and brochures are for customers. You will also need a plan just for yourself—the project plan that will take you from dream to deadline.

From Dream to Deadline

Once you've filled out Table 4-1, you have a starting point and an ending point. You'll make this dream real only once, so that means it's a project. You can complete the project plan in three steps:

▶ *Decide when the dream will be real and set a deadline.* Look at the deadline from two perspectives. From a business perspective, plan to be ready two months before the busy season or the time to really make money. That way, if you run behind schedule, you'll still make the big day. From a project perspective, make sure you are giving yourself and your team enough time to do all the work, even while keeping your current business going.

▶ *Define the gaps between where you are now and where you want to be by creating a target diagram,* as you see in Figure 4-1.

▶ *Create a project plan* using Chapters 6 through 12.

The target diagram is a very useful tool for creating a clear picture of the path to your dream. You'll see an example in Figure 4-1. At the center, you put your dream or opportunity. On arrows pointing toward the dream, you define

Figure 4-1. A sample target diagram

each piece of work, problem, or issue between where you are now (outside the circle) and where you want to be (the target, your dream). Each arrow is one gap to close, one part of your project plan.

Thinking visually opens up the mind and helps us sort things out when there are a lot of different things to do. Thinking about gaps—defining where we are now and where we want to be—clears the mind of blame and focuses on the job to be done. Use a target diagram to get yourself focused!

The example in Figure 4-1 is a dream coming true for me. For 12 years, I've made money by training and consulting. I'd like to make some money by sharing what I've written without having to work every day for every dollar. If I can write several books, market them, sell some additional white papers— articles on advanced topics—and automate all of that on a web site, then I'll be able to share what I know with more people and make some money without exhausting myself as a road warrior. To make that dream come true, I need to do the four arrow actions in Figure 4-1. Drawing it out like this made it

Picture your dreams; aim for your dreams.

easy to write a project plan. Then I got to work. By the time this book is in your hands, it will be done: *Project Management for Small Business Made Easy* is my eighth book. To see the results of my project—and get lots of cool tips and free stuff—go to www.qualitytechnology.com.

Dream to Goal to Reality

Now is the time to start. Draw the first draft of your target diagram right now. Fill out some of the opportunity definition tool right now. You don't have to get it all right. You don't even have to finish it.

A journey of a thousand miles begins with a single step. Take that step now. Then take one more step as you read each chapter of *Project Management for Small Business Made Easy*.

Your dreams are just a few steps away.

Conclusion: Making Your Dreams Real

Henry David Thoreau said, "If you have built castles in the air, your work need not be lost; that is what they should be. Now put the foundations under them." Committing to just one dream or opportunity and giving it a deadline is the first step in building the foundation. The second step is to make a project plan. The third step is to do the project. The fourth is to reap the rewards of your clear, focused work.

As you write the plan and do the project, you will run into problems. But—strange as this may sound—having problems isn't a problem! As long as we acknowledge each problem, accept it, and decide to deal with it—magic!—the problem becomes a project.

If you're ready to learn how to turn a problem into a project, then turn the page and read Chapter 5, Problems and Solutions.

Chapter 5

Problems and Solutions

SOME PEOPLE LIKE TO HIDE FROM PROBLEMS. *THEY CALL THEM* ISSUES OR *concerns*. I like to be more straightforward. A problem is a problem. And when I recognize that, I put it on a schedule to fix it. As soon as I do that, the problem becomes a project.

In Chapter 1, we said a good project manager is like a doctor—we diagnose problems before jumping in to fix them. In this chapter, you will learn:

▶ To understand the different parts of a problem

▶ Several tools to investigate and define problems

▶ How to turn a problem into a project

▶ How to make sure your solution works

What Is a Problem?

If I have an old car sitting in my garage and it doesn't run, then the fact that it doesn't run is not a problem. But if I own only one car and it doesn't run, then that's a problem. A problem is something that gets in the way of what we want to do. If we have something we need to use and it's broken, that's a problem. If something is blocking the path to where we want to go, that's a problem.

So, the time to define our problems is after we've defined our dreams and opportunities. We set our direction in Chapter 4. Now, we're going to define the problems that get in our way and turn them into projects.

Right and Wrong Questions

There are a bunch of wrong ways to approach problems and they're all about blame. Blame asks questions about the past, but only to point fingers. "Who did this?" "Who made this mess?" Those kinds of questions don't get us anywhere.

Blame just gets in the way of finding good solutions.

Instead of asking, "Who?" if something isn't working, ask, "What?" and then ask, "Why?" "What happened?" "What's wrong?" "Why did this happen?" Those are useful questions.

Another way to avoid blame is to focus on the present and the future. Once we understand what happened, we shift from the past to the future and ask, "What can we do to fix this?" Then "Who?" can be the right question: "Who is the best person to fix this problem?" And he or she might just be the person who made the mistake.

The only reason to ask about the past is to plan the future.

The Parts of a Problem

A problem has some or all of these five parts:

- ▶ a crisis
- ▶ a symptom
- ▶ a consequence
- ▶ a cause
- ▶ a root cause

If there is a crisis, we take care of that first. Then we look at the symptom. We separate the symptom from the consequences of the problem and we evaluate the consequences. If the consequences are costly enough, then we decide the problem is worth fixing. Otherwise, we choose the least expensive solution—live with it!

If we decide to fix the problem, we look at the cause and the root cause. Understanding those will help us develop the best solution.

Let's take a closer look at each of these ideas:

- ▶ *What makes a situation a problem?* A situation is a problem only if it gets in the way of doing what we want to do. Some people can make big problems out of situations of no real consequence, making mountains out of molehills. Business problems basically come in two forms: barriers to ongoing business and barriers to realizing new opportunities.

▶ *A crisis requires urgent attention.* Sometimes, part of a problem requires immediate action: if we don't do something, things will get worse. We take care of a crisis so we can buy time to fix the problem. All crises are problems, but not all problems include a crisis.

▶ *The symptom tells us about the problem.* The symptom is something we can see or smell or measure that tells us that there is a problem. Where there's smoke (symptom), there's fire (cause). Doing something about the smoke does nothing at all. We have to look deeper than the symptom to find the cause. Then we can make a real difference.

▶ *The consequence of a problem is the unwanted results if we do nothing.* When we describe a problem, the consequence is the possible future of the problem. If we solve the problem, we won't have that unwanted consequence.

▶ *The cause is the center of the problem.* The most basic project is to define the cause of a problem and change that cause so that the problem stops happening. Sometimes there's more than one cause that we may have to fix.

▶ *The root cause is the cause of the cause.* Sometimes, we solve one problem after another, yet the problems keep coming back. It's just like pulling up dandelions: if we don't remove the whole root, dandelions will keep coming up. If we can find and dig out the root cause, then the problem will never happen again.

▶ *A permanent preventive solution puts an end to a root cause.* If we remove all the dandelion roots from our garden, then the dandelions never grow back. If we remove all the root causes of our problems from the way we work, then our problems don't come back.

When we encounter a problem, our first question should be "Is there a crisis?" If so, then take care of the crisis. If not, then examine the problem before you try to solve it. If there's no crisis, we've got some time to understand the problem and come up with a really good solution. When we can describe a problem's symptoms, consequences, and causes, we can say that we understand the problem.

Tools for Defining Problems

Table 5-1, the problem-definition tool, will allow you to sort out the pieces of a problem.

Sometimes, when we've defined the problem, there is one clear, obvious, easy solution. In that case, we should just do it. All too often, though, the situation isn't that clear. If a problem has multiple causes, we might need to fix one of the causes, some of the causes, or all of them. If a problem is really

Name of Problem:
Date:
Your name:
Company name:
Problem Description
is there a crisis? _____Yes _____No (If yes, take immediate action, then come back to complete this form.)
What are the *symptoms*? (What tells me there is a problem? What do these symptoms tell me about the problem?)
What are the *causes* of this problem? (List one or more causes.)
What are the *consequences* of this problem? (What will happen if you do nothing? List one or more consequences.)

Table 5-1. Problem-definition tool

expensive to fix, then we might be better off living with the problem and managing it rather than solving it. For example, if we have dandelions in our garden, it might be easier, cheaper, and healthier to weed the garden once a week than to dig up all the dandelion roots or use weed killer. So, instead of solving a problem, we can just bring it under management.

What Problems Are You Living With?

Take a look at your company or your office. Talk with the people on your team. Ask them and yourself, "What problems are we living with? What things do we have to take care of or fix or adjust over and over?" Write down a list of problems that you are living with, titled "Problems Under Management." Next to each problem, write down the name of the person who knows the problem best. (That's usually the person who has to fix it all the time.)

For each problem under management, give a copy of the problem-definition tool (Table 5-1) to the person who knows the problem best. Have him or her describe the problem. Then you and your team are ready for the next step, picking a good solution.

The biggest mistake that people make in defining problems is assuming that each problem has only one cause. Usually, a problem will have several causes. If we can find them all, we have a much better chance of defining a low-cost project that truly eliminates the problem.

For example, suppose you run a business installing home theater systems for your customers. Business isn't going so well and you do a customer satisfaction survey. You find your customers are not happy with your services at all. It would be silly to think that there is just one reason.

Instead, you need to do more research. Each customer had a different experience and there were probably a number of problems, some of which happened once and some of which happened several times.

When you put the list of problems together, you should organize it into three categories:

- ▶ problems from your own company, directly under your control
- ▶ problems you can influence
- ▶ problems you can't do anything about

Here is an example:

▶ *Problems directly under your control* might include "installers didn't show up on schedule," "system didn't work after the installer left," or "installers were impolite, dirty, or uncomfortable to be around."

▶ *Problems under your influence* might include "delivery of components was delayed" or "customer chose incompatible components and we didn't catch the error."

▶ *Problems you can't do anything about* might include "power failure delayed installation."

When you come up with a list of multiple causes, take care of the ones under your control first. Through better hiring, management, and training, make sure the customers are totally satisfied with your team. Then approach your vendors to solve problems with supplies and other things that you can influence. Last, create a program that acknowledges the frustration created by circumstances beyond your control and gives the customers some sort of compensation for their trouble.

Once we've defined a problem, we can ask whether we want to solve just this one problem or go after a bunch of similar problems all at once. To go after many problems at once, we will need to do more work. We'll need to understand the root cause of the problem and design a permanent preventive solution.

What is a root cause? As we've seen, problems have many causes. If we go one step further, each cause has a cause. And, of course, those causes have causes as well. We can always go back and find an earlier cause. Doing that is the first step in a root cause analysis.

The easiest way to find a root cause is to ask the question "Why?" five times. "Why was the customer dissatisfied?" "Because the installer did not show up on the right afternoon." "Why didn't the installer show up on the right afternoon?" "Because the morning installation took all day." "Why did the morning installation take all day?" "Because the installer was not trained to install the new model of TV that the morning customer ordered." "Why wasn't the installer trained before he went on the job?" "Because he was scheduled to go to training the next week." "Why did we send an installer on a job he wasn't trained to do?" "Because we don't have a system for checking specific equipment against installer training."

When we solve all the sources of a problem, our work flows to our customer and their money flows to us.

49

After five whys, we've found the root cause. And we have our solution: put in a system that tracks training and jobs so that all installers are trained for the specific jobs they are sent out to do.

The Five Whys technique drills down to the most basic cause of the problem. If we solve that problem permanently, throughout the entire company, we usually get the most improvement in the bottom line for the least cost.

From Problem to Project

Once we've named a problem and filled out the problem-definition tool, we've brought the problem under control, under management. Now, it's time to plan a solution.

As we've said, sometimes the solution is obvious once we've described the cause of the problem. But sometimes it isn't.

To pick a simple example, suppose a piece of equipment is broken. Is the solution to get it fixed or to replace it? That depends on all kinds of things, such as the nature of the problem, the cost of repair, the cost of a new machine, whether the new machine will have better features or functionality or reliability than the old one, and how much money is in your bank account this month.

Here is a process for going choosing the best solution to a problem. The general steps are in italics. This example is worked out in plain text after the italics.

1. *Picture the solution.* A piece of equipment—old or new—working at the office.
2. *Ask if you need information.* Do you need to get a price quote on repair? On a new machine? Do you need to learn about newer models? Do you need to see how much money you have available?
3. *Ask if you need expertise.* Are you and your team qualified to come up with the best solution? Remember that a lot of expertise is free these days—between vendors who will give a price quote at no charge and internet research, we can often get the know-how we need while spending little or no money and little time.
4. *List your options. Write out a clear description of each solution.* The repair will cost $2,000 and the machine will probably last two more

years. A new machine costs $6,000 and will probably last five years.

5. *Maybe make a decision. If one option is clearly better than the others, then select that one. If not, then put off the decision by including making the decision as part of the project plan.* In this case, we might delay the decision until we've learned about financing options on the new machine and the money we can make selling the old machine.

Once we have one option or several options and we know how we will make our decision, we've turned the problem into a project. Use the next six chapters to plan the project thoroughly and then carry through to success.

Which Problem Do I Tackle First?

Sometimes, we end up under a pile of problems. If we don't take them one at a time, we'll never dig our way out. But which one do we tackle first? You have two good choices. You can pick the problem with the biggest payoff first, the problem that has the biggest impact on the bottom line. Or, if you're feeling really overwhelmed, choose the smallest problem first. There's nothing like a small success to get us restarted when we're stuck.

Sometimes, we have to solve several problems to get things working. For example, if a car has no gas and flat tires, we have to fix both problems before we can use the car.

The Lesson: Line up your problems, pick one, and get going!

Conclusion: Making the Solution Work

Once we've defined the problem and chosen our solution, we make a full project plan. You'll learn to do this in Chapters 6 through 12. Then we follow the plan to success, as described in Chapters 13, 14, and 15. When we're done, we follow through to a complete and successful solution of the problem for our company or our customer.

It pays to fix your problems—and it isn't that hard.

We can understand success on a problem-solving project by remembering that a business is like a car—when we fix the part that is broken, we know it is fixed because we can use the car, continuing our trip to our destination. Just the same, if we've fixed a business problem, then the business should be working again. So it's not enough just to get a solution; we have to get the solution—and the business—working. Here are some examples of what I mean:

▶ If you need better bookkeeping, you can't just buy some new software. You have to learn how to use it, load the data, and keep your books up to date.

▶ If you buy a new piece of equipment, make sure your workers know how to use it—and use it fully and productively.

▶ New equipment needs to be reliable. Do you know how to maintain it? Do you know how to get it working after a disaster such as a flood or a fire?

When you have equipment, tools, and instructions in place and the training is completed, then your business is running well with your new solution. Congratulations! Your problem is gone and you're back at work!

Chapter 6

What Are We Making?

NOW THAT YOU'VE LEARNED HOW TO DEFINE DREAMS, OPPORTUNI-ties, and problems, it's time to pick one and plan out what we are doing in detail to make this project happen. The Project Management Institute calls this defining the *scope* of the project. Scope planning includes defining all that we are making and clarifying what we are not making. When we are done planning scope, we should have a clear picture of what we are making. Once we know what we are making, we can define how we will make it—that is, we move from describing results to describing the steps of the process, the tasks that will get the work done.

Scope definition starts with the big picture; then it works all the way down into the details. As we keep planning, we refine very precisely our description of what we are making. When we're done, we have a complete picture of what we are making and we also have a to-do list—an action plan—that will guide us in doing the work of the project.

Complete, accurate, detailed scope planning is the most important part of project planning. If we describe the scope correctly, then the action plan, the schedule, the budget, the risk plan, the quality plan, and every other part of our project plan will be good as well. If we leave something out of the scope

Many Ways of Describing Project Results

In defining scope, it is good to explain what we are doing in many different ways. Here are several ways of describing a product or service—the results of our project—and how we might make use of those descriptions:

- ▶ *Value:* A short explanation of why we are doing the project, of the benefit it will bring to customer and company. This one-sentence justification of the project makes sure we get commitment to the project.
- ▶ *Benefits:* A list of the ways that the product or service is good for the customer. This helps with marketing and sales.
- ▶ *Features:* A description of what the product or service does. This helps the customer decide if it is right for him or her.
- ▶ *Components:* A list of all the pieces of the product or service. This helps define all the steps of work we will do.
- ▶ *A system:* This shows how all the components work together. This is useful for testing and also for future repairs or modifications.
- ▶ *A set of steps of work:* This is the to-do list for our project. This is the core of the project plan that will allow us to estimate time, cost, and other factors.

The Lesson: A complete description of our project and product will make sense to everyone and give us everything we need to plan a path to success.

definition, then that item will be missing from our budget, our schedule, and everything else—and our project will be headed for trouble.

The Steps of Defining Scope

Here are the steps of defining scope, from the big picture down to the details.

1. Write a basic statement of what we are making.
2. Choose a general approach to how we will make it.
3. Draw and write a detailed description of what we are making.
4. Write a detailed *Work Breakdown Structure (WBS)*.
5. Write a detailed action plan.

Write a Basic Statement of What We Are Making

If you are launching a project to create a dream, fulfill an opportunity, or solve a problem, then you've already written this statement using the tools in

Chapters 4 and 5. If you are doing a project for a customer, then you need to take a different approach, called *requirements elicitation.*

To put it simply, requirements elicitation means finding out what your customers want—in detail. The problem is that they know what they want, but they can't put it into words easily. So, we have to figure out who our customers are, meet with them, ask questions, and write up the answer. Once we write up the answer, we show it to the customers—and anyone else who cares—and make sure that everyone understands and agrees with what we are doing.

Requirements elicitation isn't easy. Here are some of the most common challenges:

▶ *Some customers simply don't know what they want until they see it* and don't know what will work for them until they try it out and use it.

▶ *Some customers aren't available.* If we are developing a product or service for sale, we don't even know who our customers will be. We need to either let a marketing department be a substitute for our customers or develop some kind of a customer focus group.

▶ *Some customers know what they want, but can't define it unless we guide them* through the process of describing the product or service, its functionality, and its value step by step.

Make what the customers want, not what you think they want.

To define project requirements, we're going to have to find the customers and guide them through the process of telling us what will be good for them. Here is how to do requirements elicitation in six steps:

1. *Figure out who the customers are.* If there is more than one group of customers and they have different needs, answer each of the rest of the questions for each customer group.
2. *If you can, prepare a prototype, mock-up, or picture of the product* so that the customers can look at it, play with it, and tell you what they think.
3. *Make a list of questions* that you want your customers to answer.
4. *Meet with the customers,* show them what you've got, ask your questions, and write down everything. You may want to meet with them more than once.
5. *Write up a clear, detailed description of the product or service,* based on your notes from the customer meetings.

6. *Show the results to the customers* and get their approval before you launch the project.

Never Start Work on a Project Until the Customers Approve the Plan

It would be a big mistake to meet with the customers once, then write up the plan and get to work. Always show your customers the plan. You might have misunderstood something. The customers might have left something out. A careful review of the plan with the customers is essential to project success.

Choose a General Approach to How We Will Make It

As we discussed in Chapter 5, Problems and Solutions, there are many different ways of solving a problem or building a new product. We might do it in-house with our own staff, we might hire a consultant, or we might subcontract the entire job. We might fix what we have or we might buy or make something new. The second step in scope definition is to choose our basic approach. We should be careful: if you are not an expert in this area, get some advice before you decide. Choosing the wrong approach can turn a project into a disaster. For example, many homeowners and small business owners think that they can do something as well as a professional can and save some money by doing it themselves. Most of the time, that doesn't work. If it could be done better and cheaper, a professional would already know how! So it is best to either use the best—hire an expert—or learn from the best before you do it yourself.

In planning the basic approach, you'll decide whether you're fixing something old or making something new and whether you're using your own team, bringing in an expert to work with you, or contracting the job out entirely. In addition, there are two other important decisions to make—you need to define your *driver* and list the *constraints* on the project.

A driver is the single, most important direction on a project. Since my company is called Quality Technology & Instruction, quality—making each book and course as good as it can be—is the main driver on most of my projects. Other companies might focus on speed (getting the job done as soon as possible) or cost (doing it as inexpensively as possible). For each project, you choose one driver.

After you choose a driver, write up a list of constraints. A constraint is a limit on the project. For example, if the driver is quality, we might say, "Make it as good as possible, as long as it is done by the end of the year and costs under $2,000." In that case, the time limit and cost limit are constraints.

*F*ocus on one driver: highest quality, lowest cost, or earliest delivery.

Draw and Write a Detailed Description of What We Are Making

Now you are ready to write a detailed description of the product, service, or result of your project. Each detail you don't write down now will take ten times longer when, in the middle of the project, you have to stop work and figure out what you are doing. As we discussed in Chapter 1, the best project managers plan most thoroughly. A complete, detailed plan is essential when life is on the line, but it also pays off on any project.

The Institute of Electrical and Electronics Engineers has written an excellent description of a good *requirements specification*. It has these qualities:

▶ *Complete.* The whole scope is there.

▶ *Consistent.* It doesn't contradict itself.

▶ *Correct.* It contains no errors and accurately represents user requirements.

▶ *Feasible.* It can be accomplished within the time, cost, and other constraints of the project.

▶ *Modifiable.* It can be revised without getting scrambled.

▶ *Necessary.* All the information is needed for the project.

▶ *Prioritized.* Items are identified as required or, if not required, given an order of priority, so that if scope has to be reduced, we know which items to cut first.

▶ *Testable.* The items are defined well enough that the project team and/or the user can look at each of them and say if the product meets the requirement.

▶ *Traceable.* Each detail of each requirement can be traced to the customer who requested it, to each module and feature necessary for its implementation, and to its place(s) in the Work Breakdown Structure, the activity list, project plans, tests, and other records of project activity.

▶ *Unambiguous.* Each element of the specification has only one reasonable interpretation.

Although the IEEE recommended these specifically for software design specifications (in document 803.1993), I find that it helps to review any specification and every project-planning document with these qualities in mind.

Pictures and Words

The best specifications include both pictures and words and even have more than one type of picture. Think of an architect's design for a house. There will be a picture or model for potential buyers plus a description stating the number of bedrooms, the location, and other features of the home. Those are for the customers. For the construction team, there will be blueprints plus a long list of building materials and very exact engineering specifications.

The Lesson: A picture may be worth a thousand words, but your project plan will need a picture *and* a thousand words.

Write a Detailed Work Breakdown Structure (WBS)

A Work Breakdown Structure is a detailed list of all the parts of our product or service. For example, the WBS for an airplane would list one fuselage, two wings, some engines, a tail, some controls, seats, so forth and so on. The WBS includes all of the items that go into the product and only those items. It is a hierarchical list, so the detail of an engine would have a housing, a block, cylinders, pistons, and so forth. The lowest-level items in a WBS are called *work packages*. When we make each work package right and put it all together and test it, our project will be complete.

How to Write a WBS

A WBS links what we are making to how we will make it.

To write a WBS, think about the unique parts of this project first. Set aside the parts that are like ones you made on past projects. Think about the unique parts and then describe them carefully with pictures and words. We do the unique parts first because if we don't, we often forget them or don't give enough attention to those details.

After you've done that, add the ones that are more familiar. In fact, if you have plans or a WBS from a past project, you can copy the parts that are similar to what you've done before from a past project plan. Just make sure to include any changes that are different this time around.

In making a WBS, we need to remember that we have a budget and a schedule. Since a WBS should include all the work to be done, we need a section of the WBS for project management—the work we will do to make sure we deliver on time and within our budget. For example, be sure to include time for gate reviews and for the rework that might be needed if the deliverables need to be fixed after the review. We also want to make sure that we get the job done right—with quality. So we create a section of the WBS that includes all the work we will do to ensure quality—testing, quality control, and quality assurance.

Once we've broken down the work into small pieces, it becomes easy to see how we will do the work. Creating the WBS has helped us make the crucial transition from *what* we are making to *how* we will make it.

Making a Really Good WBS

Here are some tips for making an excellent WBS:

- ► *Let each person make the WBS for the work he or she will do.* People are more committed when they plan their own work. It also lets everyone contribute expertise to the project.
- ► *Walk through the WBS as a team* to clarify ideas and make improvements.
- ► *Never copy a whole WBS*—because every project is unique. But copy—and modify—parts of WBSs that are similar from past projects.

Checking the WBS

When we think the WBS is done, we should make sure it's clear and complete. Have everyone on the project look at it. Have each person walk through his or her work. Is everything there? Could each person do a good job without any further instructions? If you put it all together, would everything work or would anything be missing? Remember: every missing step in the WBS means an inaccurate budget, a schedule you can't keep, and ten times as much work to fix it later. Take the time to get it right the first time!

We get it right the first time by doing three things: checking, checking, and checking.

Write a Detailed Action Plan

In writing the WBS, we went from the top—the big picture of the whole thing we are making—down to the bottom—to each work package that describes a small, manageable part of the whole project. That is called *top-down design*, and it is the best way to bring a project under management.

Now, we're going to complete our work plan by going from the bottom up. We start with each detail—each work package—and ask, "How will I make this?" If you're working with other people on the project, assign each work package to a team member. Then say, "Write down how you're going to make this and to test it to make sure it works." Each person should create an action plan for each work package and you should read and review them all. When you review each work package, here's what you should check:

▶ *Is each step clear?* A clear step is a verb followed by a noun. For example, "draw blueprint," "write user instructions," and "assemble gearbox" are all good, clear steps.

▶ *Is there a clear starting point?* Are all the components listed? Does the worker know where he or she will get each one?

▶ *Is everything checked or tested as the work is done?*

▶ *Is all the work necessary to complete the whole work package included?*

▶ *Are all appropriate tests included?*

▶ *Does a walk-through show that this will get everything done?*

▶ *Is this the best way to do the job?*

An action plan should be so clear that if one person leaves the project, another person with appropriate skill can step in and do the job without a problem.

Working as a team, keep improving the action plan until you see that every step is written down, so that each work package will be complete and correct. Then add work packages for assembling components and testing everything as the parts come together and then more tests when it is all assembled. Be sure to include action plans for project management, such as weekly status meetings, and quality management, such as end-user testing to ensure customer delight.

When the WBS and action plan are complete, you are ready to create a detailed estimate of the time and cost, finish planning, and launch the project.

Become a Better Planner

Many people in small businesses are expert planners in their own fields. An experienced plumber or electrician can look at a job and figure out the best way to do it pretty quickly. But if you do many different types of projects, it is good to improve your planning skills. Project planning is a big subject: there are entire books on requirements elicitation and work breakdown structuring. For more tools, be sure to check out the web page that supports this book, www.qualitytechnology.com/DoneRight.

Conclusion: A Leader with a Plan

Congratulations! If you've taken your project all the way through this chapter, you've prevented most of the common causes of project failure. Most complete project failures happen either because no one has a clear sense of what the team is going to do or because some people think one thing and others think something else. If you've written down a clearly defined scope and gotten everyone to agree to it, you're past those pitfalls. Your step-by-step action plan is a road map to success.

What's the next step? In Chapter 7, Planning Time and Money, you'll learn how to estimate cost and build a schedule.

Chapter 7

Planning Time and Money

NOW THAT WE HAVE A DETAILED PLAN OF WHAT WE ARE MAKING, it's time to figure out how much it will cost, when we will do it, and how long it will take. The techniques in this chapter are not difficult, but few people take the time to really use them well. In the first section if this chapter, we'll look at the basic concepts of estimating and planning time and money. Then we'll look at detailed scheduling and preparing a budget so that you can be ready to keep track of your work, time, and money as the project moves ahead.

Allocating, Estimating, Scheduling, and Budgeting

Planning a budget and schedule is easy if we take it in small steps. Let's start by defining the most important terms:

▶ *Allocation.* When we say, "I want to spend this much money and time," we're allocating time and money. We might say, "If I can do this for under $2,000, it's worth doing." Allocation is based on what our business can give to the project. It is completely separate from *estimation*, which is a measure of what it will take to do the project.

▶ *Estimation.* Estimation is a thoughtful guess about the future. Based on our project plan, how much will this project cost? How long will it take? The types of estimation methods we use early in the project, when we have less information, are different from the methods we use later, when we know more.

▶ *Scheduling.* Scheduling is more detailed than estimation. Estimation gives us a statement of the total amount of work. Scheduling gives us a plan: what job will be done each day, each week, until all the work is done.

▶ *Budgeting.* A budget is a plan for spending money from the beginning of the project to the end.

Let's look at some key concepts about how to get allocation, estimation, scheduling, and budgeting done right.

Key Concepts

If we remember a few basic rules, we can avoid the most common problems in planning time and money:

▶ *Keep allocation and estimation separate.* Allocate based on the amount of time and money the company can reasonably spend to get project results. Estimate from the project plan. After both the allocation and the estimate are prepared, then see if the project is affordable. If not, change the plan or cancel the project.

▶ *In estimating, avoid bias.* Bias means leaning one way or the other. For example, if you say, "I have to do this for under $2,000," then you'll try to make the numbers look right. You could end up fooling yourself—telling yourself that you can do a $5,000 job for $2,000. Instead, make an honest estimate and then deal with the gap between the estimate and the allocation.

▶ *In estimating, be as accurate as possible.* Early on in a project, we don't know enough to make a very precise estimate. Instead, we should come up with a range, such as "We can finish this project in two to four weeks." As we learn more and plan the project in detail, we can make a better estimate. When we've complete the WBS and action plan that we talked about in Chapter 6, What Are We Making? we can make a precise estimate along with our schedule and budget.

Estimating is easy, but most people think they'll never get it right.

Allocate and estimate separately. Then resolve the gap.

▶ *In time estimation, separate effort and duration.* Effort is the amount of work, measured in person-hours. Duration is the total schedule, from beginning to end, in days. Estimate effort first. Then figure out duration based on how many hours people will be working.

▶ *We actually plan work, not time and money.* The time and money we spend are the results of the actions we take and the work we do. We can't simply say, "I'll spend less money; I'll take less time." We have to say, "I'll change the way I work to spend less money and take less time." And what matters, in the end, is how much work we get done, not just how much time or money we spend.

Keep these principles in mind as you learn the arts of estimation, scheduling, and budgeting.

Early Estimation

The first two questions that a business owner usually asks about a project are "How much will it cost?" and "How long will it take?" An early time and cost estimate is the project manager's first answer to those questions.

Any estimate we do before we have completed the WBS and action plan is an early estimate. Since we haven't worked out all of the details of what we will do, our estimate will be a broad range. The goal is to come up with a range so that, when the project is done, the actual cost is somewhere in the middle of the estimate range, probably on the low end. So, if we say, "This project will cost between $1,000 and $2,000," we hope that the final cost will be $1,250, but we're ready for a bit less—or a lot more.

Here are some steps for preparing a good early time estimate:

1. *Complete as much of the plan as you can.* For example, choose your basic approach to the work before preparing the estimate.
2. *Write down any decisions you haven't made.* For example, if you are planning to buy a new car, write down, "I haven't decided if I'll buy a brand new car or a used car."
3. *Make a rough list of the steps that you are going to take.* This isn't a full action plan or WBS, but it's a start.
4. *Put two columns next to the list—low estimate and high estimate.* In the low estimate column, write down the shortest amount of hours you think each task will reasonably take, and in the high estimate column, put the longest reasonable time.

5. *Add up the totals* of each column to get your low and high estimates.

You can follow a very similar process for creating a cost estimate:

1. *Complete as much of the plan as you can.*
2. *Write down any decisions you haven't made.*
3. *Make a shopping list.* What will you buy?
4. *Make a rough list of the steps that you are going to take.* This isn't a full action plan or WBS, but it's a start.
5. *Put two columns next to the list—low estimate and high estimate.* In the low estimate column, write down the least amount of money you think each task will reasonably cost, and in the high estimate column, put the largest amount of money.
6. *Add up the totals* of each column to get your low and high estimates.

Time Is Money

If you've ever said, "I did it myself and it didn't cost me a cent!" you were fooling yourself. You are worth something and so is your time. If you earn a salary, your time is worth your hourly rate plus 50 percent for benefits and other overhead. If you run your own business, your time is worth what you could have been doing if you hadn't been doing this project. When planning a project, consider the cost of your own time.

The Lesson: It is a mistake to think that your time or the time of your staff doesn't count as money. Often, we are better off hiring an expert to do a project and spending our time making money some other way.

How do we decide how long each item on our list will take or how much money it will cost? Here are some approaches:

▶ *Do some research.* Take a few minutes to look up prices or to ask someone who's done this kind of work before.

▶ *Estimate based on the steps of a past project.* Don't compare with an entire past project, but do compare each work package with work packages in a past project. Do it intelligently. Don't just copy the numbers. Instead, ask, "What's different this time? Is there anything that would make it take more or less time? Cost more or less?"

▶ *When in doubt, guess.* If you guess several items, your guesses will average out pretty accurately, as long as you do a high and low estimate on each guess.

The high and low estimates are important. If you don't do both, you'll be either consistently optimistic or consistenly pessimistic.

I Can't Afford This!

What do we do if, after we create our estimate, we find that the project will cost too much or take too long? We have a gap between what we are willing to allocate and what we estimate it will take to do the job.

What we shouldn't do is sweep the problem under the rug. Instead, let's face it squarely by asking these questions:

- ▶ Can we find the extra money or time?
- ▶ Can we come up with a different basic approach that will cost less, deliver sooner, or deliver more value?
- ▶ If we delay the project to a different time, will that make a difference?
- ▶ If we assume our estimates are correct, what do we really want to do—go ahead or drop the project? Which will leave us better off in the end?

Asking these questions, we make a clear *go or no-go decision.*

This short introduction will give you a good start at estimating a project. If you want more detailed instructions, plus spreadsheets and tools, go to www.qualitytechnology.com/DoneRight.

Detailed Scheduling

We create a detailed schedule from the WBS and action plan we wrote in Chapter 6, What Are We Making? For simple projects, we can write this out on paper or with a word processor. For more advanced projects, you might want to use project management software, which automates a lot of the tasks, such as tracking people's available time. In this section, we'll introduce the basic ideas that work with any tools.

To create a project schedule, follow these steps:

1. Make sure your action plan is complete and correct.
2. Resolve any open decisions or unanswered questions.
3. Assign each work package or task to a specific person.
4. Decide if each person will work on the project full time or what hours each will be available.
5. Have each person come up with a single, final estimate of how long each task will take, somewhere between the low estimate and the high one. Have them use low estimates for familiar work and high estimates for newer tasks.

6. Put the tasks in order. Some tasks can be done in any order. Others have to come first. If the output of one task is the input of another task, make sure to put the first task before the second.

7. Include time for testing each output. Never plan to go ahead on a next step until you are sure the prior step was done right.

8. Allow time for things like paint drying or ovens warming up, where no work is being done, but time has to pass anyway. This is called *lag time*.

9. Check people's calendars for holidays, vacation, and other work that might get in the way of the project.

10. Pick a start date and work forward, or pick an end date and work backwards, from the last task to the first.

11. Assign each task to a date. Include time for status meetings, tests, gate reviews, and rework.

12. Review the schedule with each team member, making any changes or corrections.

A schedule simply describes who will do what when.

Detailed Budgeting

A budget is actually pretty easy to prepare. On a project, we spend money on two things: people's time and things we buy. To prepare the detailed budget, take these steps:

1. Assign a dollar value to each person's time. A good rule is to take his or her hourly wage and add 50 percent for benefits plus cost of the office and such. If the person has an annual salary, divide it by 1,500 to get the hourly wage, then add the 50 percent. (That's based on a 30-hour workweek, but we're measuring productive hours here, so that's realistic.)

2. Add up each person's total time and then multiply it by his or her hourly rate. Add up all those totals for the total cost of time on the project. Be sure to include yourself.

3. Review your shopping list against the completed WBS and action plan. Revise it, adding anything else you need to buy.

4. Do some research and get actual prices for your shopping list. Don't forget to include sales tax, shipping, and such.

5. Check for incidental expenses such as gas, travel expenses, or lunch for the team, and include those.

6. Add it all up.

We spend money for people's time and for the things we need to buy.

You can link your budget to your calendar, so that you know how much money you expect to spend each week of the project. Some projects spend more money at the beginning or the end, while others spend steadily all the way through.

Conclusion: Ready to Stay on Track

We've planned work, time, and money—and that's the core of the project plan.

We now know what we're making, when we're doing each task, and how much time and money each task will take. At least, we have a plan for it. One thing we can be sure of—no project ever goes exactly according to plan. To give ourselves a better shot at success, we'll plan for quality in Chapter 8, plan for risks and unexpected problems in Chapter 9, and then plan how to work with our team and everyone else in Chapter 10. Of course, these activities take time and money, so we'll be adjusting our schedule and budget as we improve the plan over the next several chapters.

Once we launch the project, we will use this plan to track progress, making sure we get work done on schedule and within our budget. We'll track as we go, so that we can make course corrections promptly if we get off track.

Getting Better and Better

The first time you make an estimate for a project, you may not do that good a job. Don't feel bad: at least you tried. To be honest, many project managers don't even try—and they end up in hot water.

At the end of each project—or even at each gate review—be sure to ask yourself *why* your estimate is working or is off target. Write down the answer and keep it with your instructions for estimating a project.

The next time you launch a project, review those notes and you'll do better.

Chapter 8

Making It Good

NOW IT'S TIME TO TALK ABOUT QUALITY. IN FACT, THE SOONER WE talk about quality, the better. Many people think that we have to focus on getting the job done and we don't have time to get it done right. The opposite is true. When we don't get a job done right, we get it done wrong. Then either we lose money and time doing a lot of rework or we lose customers because our competitors did it right when we didn't. The opposite of quality is error—and error is expensive.

However, if we plan quality in from the beginning, it actually costs less to do a good job than it would cost to do a bad job. There are three reasons for this, three points that are the core of project quality management:

▶ *A good design costs no more than a bad design.* During planning, it costs very little to get it right. A blueprint costs just the same for a new office we will love as for a new office we can't work in. But, if we go with the bad design, we'll pay the price later.

▶ *Error is inevitable, and the sooner we deal with it, the better.* People make mistakes. The only thing we can do is bring errors under management, so that the mistakes don't end up in our products and services.

Quality management brings errors under management. We focus on preventing error. When we can't prevent them, we try to remove them as soon as possible. The earlier we get rid of errors, the less they will cost us.

Focus on quality from the start. Good design plus good process equals great results.

▶ *Improving process improves all our results.* Quality management puts the focus on process—that is, we improve *how* we do our work. When we improve the quality of our processes, we work smarter. When we work smarter, we do a better job, completing more in less time for less money. So, by focusing on the quality of our work processes, we actually increase the scope we can deliver, improve the quality of results, and reduce time and cost as well. The end result is we deliver a better product on time (or early!) and under budget.

The best project quality management is done in five steps:

▶ *Define quality.* When we build our scope statement, we should ask, "What makes it good?"

▶ *Plan for quality.* Using quality control, quality assurance, and effective gate reviews, we find smart ways of working that deliver the best results at the lowest cost on the shortest schedule.

▶ *Control quality* to make sure that the product is what it is supposed to be.

▶ *Ensure quality* from the beginning to the end of the project.

▶ *Deliver quality* to ensure customer delight.

We'll talk about the first two of these—defining and planning for quality—in this chapter. Quality control and quality assurance will be the topics of Chapter 16, Quality: Eliminate Error. And you'll learn how to deliver quality in Chapter 20, Deliver Delight. But let's begin with some simple quality basics.

Simple Quality Basics

Everyone makes mistakes. But we want to bring errors under management and to prevent or get rid of as many errors as we can. How do we do that?

▶ *Stay motivated.* Believe we can do a good job and find joy in doing it.

▶ *Pay attention* and teach your team to pay attention. People make fewer errors when we are attentive to our work.

▶ *Catch assumptions.* When we assume something and it isn't true, costly mistakes creep in. Say assumptions aloud or write them down. Check them with your team. Make sure that what you're thinking makes sense.

▶ *Check one another's work.* Since we all make mistakes and it's hard to see our own mistakes, we can really do quality work only if someone else can check that work with us. Have your team check your work. Then ask if you can check theirs. Make it an impersonal rule—everything goes past two pairs of eyes before it leaves the office.

Quality comes from teamwork plus individual excellence.

▶ *Keep the checking independent.* If people check their own work or if the systems for checking work are the same as the systems for doing work, then assumptions creep into both the work process and the checking process. Then work passes tests, but fails in reality because our assumptions were wrong.

▶ *Review frequently.* In addition to doing good work all the way through, create gate reviews to check work frequently.

▶ *Allow time for checking and fixing.* Build into your project plan time and money for testing, fixing, and retesting.

Defining Quality

The biggest challenge to defining quality is that people will tell you that you shouldn't spend so much time planning, that you should just get to work. But the truth is that high quality from the beginning saves money. Many people think that quality is expensive. The opposite is true: mistakes are expensive. When we focus on quality from the beginning, we can make fewer mistakes, reducing total project cost and shortening the schedule. We deliver better results with less rework, sooner, while spending less money.

Don't think for your customer. Listen to your customer.

The basic process for defining quality was described in Chapter 6, What Are We Making? To add the element of quality, we change the question from "What are we making?" to "What will make it good?" We need to be realistic when we do this. We say to the customer, "Tell us what will make it good, and we'll put as much of that in as time and money allow." Within that framework, let the customer dream. Take notes so you can plan to make your customer's dream a reality. There is no more rewarding way to do business than that.

Don't Write a Blank Check

Even with a focus on quality, we can do only so much given the time and money available for the project. If you just ask, "What makes it good?" you can end up writing a blank check and setting the client's expectations way too high. Instead, create a reasonable frame for the size of the project you are doing. Give the client some options. Then, in that framework, open up a discussion of how to make it as good as it can be.

As you follow the requirements elicitation process from Chapter 6, add these elements to define quality and prepare for successful quality management:

▶ *Collaborate with your customer.* Cultivate an attitude of working together to do the best we can do.

▶ *Keep the team focused on quality.* Get each person excited about doing really great work.

▶ *Communicate, check, and document.* Most errors in quality creep in because we *assume* we understood what someone meant. Check everything more than once. Make sure you're on the same page and you share the same understanding. And then write it down—in detail.

Define features that add benefits. Then make a product that delivers those features.

The key to defining quality is to connect the user benefits that have value to the technical functions that make the product or service work. Customers gain value and experience quality when the tool is right for the job and everything runs smoothly from beginning to end. So we design quality in from the top down, defining what adds benefit for the customer and then making sure it works the way it is supposed to.

Everything I've said here works just the same way for an internal project inside your company as it does when you're doing work for your customers. It is even the same if you're doing this project just for yourself. Treat yourself and your company as a customer. Make sure that any project—even an internal one—will deliver hassle-free benefits.

Make the connection from value to benefits to features to specifications and write that down in your plan. When you've done that, you've defined quality. Then you're ready to plan for quality.

When you've defined the quality of the product or service—the project results—bring quality definition to a close by doing the following:

Getting Better at Being Good

There's an old-fashioned value that underlies quality—*humility*. These days, humility is a willingness to learn. We can learn from four sources:

▶ **Our own successes.** If we are humble enough to realize that doing something right once means we won't always get it right, then we write down our good methods so that we can succeed again and again.

▶ **Our own mistakes.** If we are willing to look closely at our mistakes without blame, then we can see what we did wrong and change our methods to do better next time.

▶ **The successes of others.** In every industry, there are best practices to learn. Take other people's good ideas and make them work for you!

▶ **The mistakes of others.** If we are humble enough to realize that we will make the same mistakes other people make, then we can learn from where others have slipped and get ahead.

The Lesson: If we want to do better, we can learn from everyone and everything we do.

Assumptions are the death of quality.

▶ Write up, review, and get commitment on a detailed product description that defines value, benefits, features, and technical specifications.

▶ Ask, "What will the customer need to be able to use this well?" Include instructions, training, and anything else that will make this work.

▶ Consider project factors other than the resulting product. What delivery date, budget, work schedule, and ways of working will make this a quality experience for the project team?

Add all of this to your plan.

What doesn't get written down gets forgotten.

Planning for Quality

Once we have a good design and a basic project plan, we can improve that plan—reducing project cost, shortening the schedule, and reducing the risk of failure—by building quality into the plan. Review the simple quality basics at the beginning of this chapter and then add these elements to your project plan.

▶ *Review every plan and document.* Make sure everything is clear. Ask yourself, "If I set this project aside for six months and did it later, could I read this plan and know exactly what to do?" If there is a team on the project, make sure every member is equally clear about what needs to be done.

▶ *Test everything*. As each component is built, test its features and functionality. As you put the whole product or service together, test features. Then go beyond that. Test robustness and reliability. Will this thing work when the rubber hits the road? Will it last a long time? Then, with the help of the customer, test benefits. Are you and the customer confident that the project results will add value for the customer—internal or external—for a long time to come? If not, fix it now.

▶ *Design tests before you do the work*. If we design our tests after we start working, we increase the chances of letting errors slip through.

▶ *Check everything using a buddy system*. No one can see all of his or her own mistakes. Part of human nature is to see things a certain way—to read what we thought we wrote and to see what we thought we saw. Make it a policy—with no blame—that everyone's work gets checked by someone else as the project goes along.

▶ *Triple-check everything at the gate*. Gate reviews are an excellent way to ensure quality. We catch errors before they move on to the next stage, where they cost ten times as much to fix.

▶ *Plan enough time for testing, rework, and retesting*. Don't assume that all tests will go well. Allow time to find and fix problems and then to recheck to make sure everything is good before the product goes to the customer.

▶ *Use the right people for testing*. Some tests require a technical expert. Others require an experienced customer or user. Make sure the right people will be available to do the right tests at the right time.

▶ *Keep getting better*. During the project, use every gate review and every error you discover as a chance to find root causes, implement permanent preventive solutions, and add to your lessons learned.

Conclusion: Taking the High Road

For some businesses, quality is an option. Maybe you want to focus on being the least expensive provider or doing the fastest jobs, rather than delivering the best. If that's the case, then you still benefit by focusing on the quality of your processes—by working smarter to achieve your goals.

But maybe you just want to get by and do a good enough job, instead of a great job. That's OK, too. But I think you're missing out on two things. First of all, you'll face a real challenge if a competitor comes along who does a better job than you do. And, more important, you're missing out on what I've found is one of the biggest joys in life. There is real joy in doing excellent work and real joy in getting better and better at what we do.

Quality brings joy to our work and success to our customers.

I learned that when I was 16 years old, from a pizza-shop owner named Giorgio. I loved pizza and I went hunting for the best pizza in Washington, DC. It was at Giorgio's. He used good ingredients. He loved what he did. He made each pizza with care. When Giorgio left the city and sold his business, I learned a valuable lesson. The people who bought his business kept his equipment, his recipe, and his ingredients. But they just didn't care about pizza. Giorgio's pizza got better every day, because he kept caring. The new owners made a pizza that just wasn't worth eating.

I hope you'll focus on quality, doing better every day for your customer and your business.

Chapter 9

Making Sure the Job Gets Done

BY NOW, OUR PLAN PROBABLY SEEMS PRETTY NEAR PERFECT. AND IT IS very good—as far as it goes. So now we have to pay attention to the stuff we can't plan for. In Chapter 8, we saw how we bring errors under control with quality management. Here in Chapter 9, we make sure the job gets done by bringing uncertainty under control with risk management.

If there's one thing that we can be sure of, it is that the future is uncertain. That means things will not always go as planned. In project risk management, we face that uncertainty and deal with it.

We could say that project risk management involves expecting the unexpected, but it is more than that. We need to expect the unexpected, but then we also need to plan for it and then do something about it. And we also need to be ready for events that are unexpected in spite of all of our planning. This gives rise to some basic ideas of risk management:

- ▶ About the only thing we can be sure of is that things will not go exactly according to plan.
- ▶ We are better off thinking of what might happen and preparing for it than we are being caught off guard.

▶ We can prepare a risk plan including a list of risks. We can make allowances for risks in the project schedule and budget.

▶ We can use the risk plan to track the status of risks during the project, check for risk events daily or weekly, and bring risk under control.

▶ The uncertain future includes possible unexpected good events, called *beneficial* or *positive* risks, as well as *negative* risks, which are problems for our project.

*U*nexpected events are sure to happen. Are you ready for them?

How Risky Is Your Project?

Some projects are riskier than others. Even before you complete the plan, you should think about how risky the project is, that is, how likely it is to get into trouble, to cost more, to take longer, or even to fail altogether. There is one key question to ask: How new is the project work to the team who will be doing it?

You can expand this question by asking:

▶ How experienced is each team member? Do we have proven successes and failures? Have we learned from our experiences?

▶ Are we using any new methods or tools? If so, do we need extra time for testing or training?

▶ Is there any constraint—such as a tight deadline, an immovable date for an event, or a strict budget limit—that limits our flexibility and makes the project harder?

▶ Is this type of work, in general, high risk?

Think this through and write down your thoughts. The riskier the project, the more time you should spend on careful planning in general and on risk management in particular.

The Lesson: The newer the project, methods, and tools are for your team, the riskier the project will be.

Here are some simple things we can do to manage risk and increase the chances of success:

▶ *Teach every member of the team to pay attention to risk and to inform you of any risk to project success.* Risks are almost always easier and less expensive to deal with when identified early. Make sure your team knows to think about risk and talk about risk.

▶ *List risks and then evaluate each risk and decide what to do about it.* We'll show you the steps in this chapter.

▶ *When things go wrong, ask, "Why?" and "Can it happen again?"* Some of the trickiest risks are small problems that happen over and over again. Looking closely at small problems, we can fix the root causes before small problems pile up into a disaster.

▶ *Watch out for little things that go wrong again and again.* They will snowball out of control and bury your project.

▶ *Manage risk throughout the project* by making it part of the weekly or daily status meeting.

The Project Management Institute has developed an elaborate project risk management system for major businesses. For small businesses, however, we need a simple, practical way to do just four processes:

▶ **Risk identification:** Figure out what could go wrong, and write it down.

▶ **Risk analysis:** Identify the likelihood and consequences of each risk, and prioritize the risks.

▶ **Risk response planning:** Get ready for what might happen, item by item.

▶ **Risk monitoring and control:** Throughout the project, check up on the risks and update the risk control plan at each daily or weekly status meeting.

For a small project, the first three processes can all be done in one meeting. Here is a simple way to manage risk on our projects to make sure that we get it done right!

Risk Identification: Listing the Risks

R isk identification is proactive worry.

We start with knowing that something could go wrong, that something unexpected could happen. We ask, "What could that be?" Then we write down the answer. The best time to hold a major risk-planning meeting is shortly after the activity list is done. We should pay attention to risk before that, but we cannot make a thorough list of risks until we know the project activities. At that point, our goals are clear and we know the details of our work plan. Our focus is positive and we want to keep it that way.

Risk planning means looking at what could go wrong to make sure that things go right. We don't want a doom-and-gloom session; we want a sense that we can handle uncertainty with good planning, attention to risk, and appropriate, timely action.

Here are ways of asking what unexpected events could happen, of asking what could go wrong or unexpectedly right, of expecting the unexpected. Be sure to have someone writing down the answers as your team brainstorms with these questions.

▶ Review the WBS, the activity list, and the list of items we plan to purchase and ask, "What could keep us from getting what we need and doing a good job?"

▶ Ask, "What are we getting from outside the team? Who are we depending on outside the team? What would happen if they don't deliver?"

▶ Ask, "What have we never done before? What areas are difficult for us?"

▶ Ask, "What has gone wrong on other projects that could happen again here?"

Write down your assumptions. Every assumption is a risk.

▶ Finally, ask, "What could go unexpectedly right? What could make the project easier, get it done sooner or at lower cost, give us a better result?" List those positive risks, too.

The result of this meeting is a list of risks, formally called a *risk register*.

Who Are You Counting On?

One of the most important ideas in project risk management has a fancy name: *external dependency*. But it's a very simple idea. Any time you count on getting anything from anyone outside the team, that person might not get you what you need when you need it. That is a project risk. The key words here are *anyone* and *anything.* There are many external dependencies on every project. Here is a thorough list of stakeholders to consider to get you started.

▶ *Customers* must provide information for the requirements specification, answers to questions, and review and testing with approvals or specific corrections for each document and component at every review gate. In some cases, customers must make timely payments to launch the project or keep it going.

▶ The *project sponsor* has to provide money and ensure support throughout the project.

▶ *Senior executives* have to provide people, answers to questions, and resolutions to conflicts.

> ▶ *Vendors* are providing products that must be delivered on time and meet specifications.
> ▶ *Consultants* should be included in the project team and their work should be on the project schedule. Until they are fully integrated with the team—if ever—we should still consider their deliverables external dependencies.
> ▶ *Regulatory agencies* may need to provide permits to allow work to proceed.
>
> Note that the word *anything* is very broad. A project can be delayed when a customer forgets to call you at the end of a gate review and say, "You're doing a great job, keep going." So, *anything* includes project components, review and approval, answers to questions, money—whatever information, person, or item is needed to do the next jobs on the project schedule.
>
> *The Lesson:* In building a list of external dependencies, don't just look at vendors. Look at everyone, especially the customers, and ask about everything, including answers, permits, and approvals.

Good News Can Be Hard to Manage

It's important to prepare for positive risks. Even good news will throw off your schedule and your budget.

Here is an example from some volunteer work I'm doing as I write this book. I'm helping the local chapter of the Project Management Institute (PMI) create a symposium—a day of professional development, including learning and job opportunities. The day had been set for August. Then a major company that provides project management training offered to bring a class to our town and have us co-sponsor the event. That would bring in a lot of money and a lot more people. Good news! But their date was October. We had to reschedule our event and change a lot of our plans. The co-sponsorship is a great opportunity, but it required a lot of preparation and planning.

The Lesson: Think of what good things might happen, too. Even positive risks require changes to our project plan.

Of course, anyone can suggest additions to the list of risks at any time and everyone should add anything that may be headed our way. The risk list grows and changes throughout the project.

In our first big risk meeting, once we have our initial risk list, we are ready to do risk analysis and risk response planning. In fact, we can do all of them in one meeting.

Risk Analysis

We now want to describe each risk, so that we will be able to manage it. There are six things we want to do for each risk:

- **Name** the risk.
- Describe the **consequence** of the risk. The consequence is what will happen if the risk event occurs and we don't do anything about it.
- Define the risk **trigger**. The trigger is the sign that the risk event is likely to happen or is starting to happen.
- Determine the **likelihood** of the risk. Likelihood is our best guess as to whether this will probably happen or just might happen.
- Estimate the **significance** of the risk event. This is a rating of the severity of the consequence.
- Describe **options for managing** the risk before or when it happens.

Likelihood and consequence are independent of one another. For example, rain may be very likely for the day of the housewarming party, but it is of little consequence for an indoor party. On the other hand, it is unlikely that the party host will get sick, but if he does, we'd have to cancel the party—the worst possible consequence. We can rate likelihood on a scale of 1 to 3 (low, medium, and high) or 1 to 5 (very low, low, medium, high, and very high). We rate consequence from 0 to 1, with 1 meaning project failure or cancellation and a number between 0 and 1 indicating the increased cost, delay in time, or loss of some scope or quality.

"Oops! I thought that might happen" is risk identification—but it isn't risk management.

Risk Response Planning

Once a risk is on our list, we have to decide what we're going to do about it—our risk management options. By putting it on the list, we've *accepted* the risk under management, that is, we've committed to keeping track of it and doing something about it. *Risk acceptance* is not passive; it is very active. In addition to accepting the risk, we can also do one or more of these:

- We can **mitigate** a risk. That means reducing its likelihood or reducing its consequences. These are two separate actions and we can do both. For example, we can reduce the likelihood of not getting the right construction supplies for a building project by identifying two suppliers. We can reduce the consequences by having an alternate schedule for the work if no supplies are available.

▶ We can **avoid** a risk by changing our plans so that the risk cannot possibly happen at all. For example, if our project originally involves travel, we avoid the risks associated with travel if we arrange to work remotely, so we don't have to travel at all. Of course, avoiding one risk usually means adding other risks.

▶ We can **transfer** the risk, for example, by getting insurance. Risk transference is not that important for most projects. When we transfer a risk, someone else foots the bill, but the project still gets into trouble or fails. However, it is important in some industries. For example, in the movie business, producers, directors, and other professionals are *bonded*. This means that an insurance company ensures that they can complete a project of a certain size on budget. If they don't, the insurance company will foot the extra bill—up to a point defined in the bonding policy. A professional gets bonded based on a proven track record. If everyone making a movie—or even an expensive TV commercial—is bonded, it is a sign that risk of project failure is significantly reduced.

Table 9-1 is an example of a risk list—or risk register—showing some of the risks for a housewarming party. A sample of a complete risk plan is available at www.qualitytechnology.com/DoneRight.

Table 9-1 shows how the risk list might look at the end of planning. The risk list is a living document. Each week, we add new risks that we think of or encounter, we cross off risks that don't happen, and we implement our mitigation strategies as needed and note that in the plan.

Risk Monitoring and Control

When we've completed our list of risks, we've completed project risk planning and we're ready to keep risk under control throughout the project. We keep risk under control by doing four things during the project:

▶ **Review the risk list** at every daily or weekly status meeting.

Risk Name	Consequence	Trigger	Likeli-hood	Signifi-cance	Management Option
Illness of host	Cancel party	Feel sick	Low	−1.0	• Accepted. • Mitigate by reducing likelihood—stay healthy, avoid stress.
Farmers' market rained out	Can't get best ingredients	Rain the day before	Low	−0.2	• Accepted. • Mitigate by reducing consequence—have alternate recipes ready.
Find a musician	Positive risk—add live music to the party	Meet a musician we really like	Low	+0.3	• Accepted. • Increase chances by going out to hear live music. • If it happens, announce on web site, add to invitation if time allows, adjust party budget.

Table 9-1. Sample risk list: Some risks for a housewarming party

▶ **Have everyone on the team keep an eye out for trouble** and talk about what is going on.

▶ **Reduce risk through good communications** by letting everyone—especially vendors, customers, and others who are involved in the project only occasionally—know how important it is to deliver things on time and do things right the first time.

▶ **Periodically review** the whole schedule and plan. Look for small things that make you lose an hour here and an hour there. These kinds of things are too small to be on your risk list—they're below the radar—but they can add up to a missed deadline or even failure of the project.

If you manage the risks, the team can get the work done.

Conclusion: If It Doesn't Go Wrong, It Will Go Right

Risk management is both a process and an attitude. This chapter shows you the process. The attitude is one of realistic optimism. Things can go right—but it takes devoted work and attention. Good risk management lets us know if we're off course, so we can get back on course before we crash the project.

Now that we've planned for what goes wrong, let's turn to Chapter 10, Teamwork and Communications, where we'll look at how to get the right people doing the right job—and *getting it done right!*

Chapter 10

Teamwork and Communications

O NE DEFINITION OF A SUCCESSFUL PROJECT IS THE RIGHT PEOPLE doing the right job. From that perspective, our job as project managers is to define the right job clearly, get the right people together, keep them focused on the job, and keep everything else out of their way. If we bring all aspects of the project under control, we manage the project and we work with the people through leadership, coaching, and facilitation. That's the recipe for herding cats!

I work with an approach I call *Team Success*™. The key is to combine good teamwork with a focus on goals. Good teamwork eliminates hassles, reducing errors and keeping us efficient. But without clear goals, teamwork is just fun rah-rah that doesn't help the business. The project plan provides the focus so that the team has a good time doing good work that helps our business and our customers.

The Project Management Institute formally calls the topic of this chapter *Project Human Resource Management and Project Communications Management*. We can simply think of it as teamwork and communications. Our topics include:

We control project work; we cooperate with the project team.

- ▶ Getting the right team
- ▶ Defining jobs clearly
- ▶ Supporting self-management
- ▶ Supporting effective team communications

Project Leadership

Gordon Bethune became CEO of Continental Airlines in 1994, when it was headed for its third bankruptcy and rated as the worst major airline in America. In his book, *From Worst to First,* he describes how he turned Continental around in two years, making it the best airline in the country, according to federal statistics and independent rating agencies. He did it using the same team of 37,000 people who were making it the worst airline only two years earlier. It is an excellent story of goal-oriented team leadership. Bethune says that a manager's job is to define the job clearly, get the right people for the job, get out of their way, and keep everything else out of their way.

Although we call it project management, our real job is project *leadership*. Each project is unique, and setting new, unique direction is leadership, not management.

The Lesson: Take control of the situation and lead your team to success.

Getting the Right Team

In a small business, getting the right team usually means taking yourself and the people you have and making them into the right team. Usually, but not always. Actually, we have three practical options:

- ▶ *Use the team we have,* learning and providing training if needed.
- ▶ *Contract the job out to experts.* For example, if you're buying a second building and renovating it to open a new location, you'll probably hire a general contractor, instead of trying to build the building yourself.
- ▶ *Use our team, but get some outside expertise.* This is a great option that we don't use nearly enough.

In this section, I'm talking about teams. But everything I say applies to a team of one, if you're doing the project yourself. And, in project management, if we bring in a part-time contractor or expert, that person is part of the team, whether or not he or she is on our payroll.

We have to begin with the clear project plan we've built using the tools in Chapters 4 through 9. After that, we review the action plan to determine what skills are needed to do the job. Then we work with the team we have to evaluate their skills in terms of the job to be done. We do a gap analysis, finding out what skills, if any, are missing.

Sometimes, we're lucky and our team has all the skills—all the proven, successful experience—to get the job done. That usually happens if the project is not unique, not that different from work that the team has done before. In that case, we have our team and the challenge is then to schedule the work around other projects and routine work and things that we need to do.

When people lack skills, don't blame. Instead, help them get the skills.

Sometimes, though, we find that there is a gap, that some knowledge or some skill is missing from the team. Our first thought should be: closing this gap will take time and money. It also adds risk, because closing the gap can be done only with one of two options:

▶ *Someone on the team learns something new.* In that case, he or she will be doing it for the first time on this project, and there is always the risk of making a mistake.

▶ *We bring in an expert.* In that case, the new person on the team is an unknown factor. What if he or she turns out not to be reliable or is unable to work well with our team?

Our best bet is to define the gap clearly and close it early. Through research or training or hiring an expert or consultant, we get the knowledge we need.

Iteration, Course Correction, and Plan, Do, Check, Act

There are three ideas underlying the approach in this chapter.

▶ *Iteration* means doing something over and over again. So, we define each gap and close it, until there are no more gaps.
▶ *Course correction* means frequently checking our course and adjusting to move in the right direction. We'll talk about this more in Chapter 13, Keeping Everything on Track.
▶ *Plan, Do, Check, Act* (PDCA) is a valuable problem-solving technique from quality management that we discuss fully in Chapter 16, Quality: Eliminate Error.

The Lesson: Find what's wrong, then fix what's wrong, over and over, until the wheel is spinning true.

We do this for each gap between the team skills and the skills needed for the project. Then we reassess the whole set of skills: do we have what we need now? And we assess if we need to do anything to pull in any new team members. Then we change our action plan to include the new people and skills. We have to coordinate training time for the team or the availability of new people with the project schedule and adjust the project schedule. Then we reassess risk. Are all the risks clear? Is the level of risk for the whole project acceptable? If so, we're ready to go. If not, we take whatever corrective action is necessary.

Once we have good people with the right skills, we have the resources for the project. However, those resources have to work together well. The next three sections talk about how we can make that happen. But we can't do it alone. Just as we work with the team, the team has to work with us.

Just recently, I met Bruce Runcie, the owner of Rose City Estate Gardens, a small landscaping business that focuses on special projects. He's been in the business over 25 years and he's defined the qualities that make someone a good worker, good team player, and potential right-hand man or woman. Here are the five qualities he said were essential, with the acronym *HIRAST*:

▶ *Honesty.* Teamwork requires that people obey laws and rules and also that we be truthful with one another.

▶ *Interest.* Each of us has to care about the job and want to improve in the type of work we are doing. It won't work if this job is just a way-station onto something different.

▶ *Reliability.* Each team member must be willing to show up and do the work and to keep the commitments necessary for the job to be done and for the business to succeed.

▶ *Attitude.* A positive attitude and concern for the customer are essential.

▶ *Skill or Teachability.* The person must have the necessary skills for the job. Or, if all four other elements are present and the person is willing and able to learn, that can work as well.

Our best bet is to hire people with these qualities. If we don't, then we'll have some degree of hassle every day as they work with us. When we're working on projects, this kind of hassle is particularly difficult, for two reasons. First of all, projects are unique, so people need to be willing to grow and learn to make a project succeed. Second, projects have deadlines, and the hassles that come with people lacking the HIRAST qualities make it very hard to keep the work flowing smoothly on schedule. If we are running a project and falling into perpetual hassles or things aren't getting done on time, we should check our team members and ourselves against the HIRAST list. If we find a gap, we'll need to either close it or work around it. Sometimes, we've dropped the ball from burnout or exhaustion. Sometimes, talking about these issues and making a commitment to a renewed effort works. Sometimes, we have to either ask someone to leave the team or just live with the problem and work around it as best as we can.

Defining Jobs Clearly

If the team members are willing to do the work, then it's our job to work with them so that they know what to do. We start with the WBS and action plan from Chapter 6, What Are We Making? Working with each team member, we make the job clear at the detailed level. At a minimum, each worker should have a clearly defined goal for each day of work. Less experienced workers may need tasks defined down to the level of one or two hours.

The key to making this work is to define tasks clearly and completely. We're talking about the basic unit of work, which is sometimes called a task, or an action, or a step. Whatever we call it, an action is something we do that leads to a clear result. The full picture of a task or action is shown in Figure 10-1, the parts of a job, also called the *I-P-O (Input-Process-Output) diagram.*

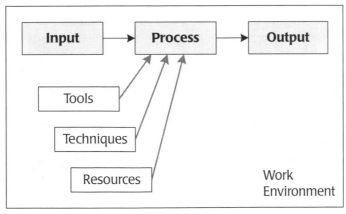

Figure 10-1. The parts of a job

When I set up a job for someone, it's my job as a manager to make sure that all seven parts of the job are in place. It is the worker's job to check that with me, make sure he or she can do the job, commit to doing it, and then deliver. Here are the seven parts:

▶ *Input*—the items that go into the process and become part of the output.

▶ *Process*—the actual activities the worker will do.

▶ *Output*—the end result: the item to be delivered, the due date, and the delivery location.

▶ *Tools*—anything the worker needs to do the job that is not used up in the process, that can be used again.

▶ *Techniques*—the written instructions for the process and also any job skills necessary to follow those instructions and do the work.

▶ *Resources*—the time spent and anything else that is used up in the process, but does not become part of the product.

▶ *Work environment.* The place the job is to be done, which must be a safe work environment and should also support effective, efficient work.

For each job, I review each of these points with the worker before the work starts. We take care of any problems we see. I also make sure that the

Each worker gets the job done right. The manager makes sure that is possible.

Too Much Information!

It may seem like discussing seven points about each task is way too much planning. And sometimes we do need less planning. Putting on a good publicity event takes less work than building a jet aircraft with over a million precision-engineered parts. We should rightsize the planning to the type of work, the experience of the worker, and the task. I've found that if I share *Team Success™* methods with a cooperative team, we do this naturally and easily. After a while, people scan the list of seven questions and say, "No problem, no problem, no problem, … wait, I don't understand this." Then we work it out.

As you do this, be sure to use the ten qualities of a good requirements specification from Chapter 6, What Are We Making? Also, keep in mind that each unnecessary step in planning may waste an hour, but each hour of planning you should do and don't will cost you ten hours of project work time.

The Lesson: Start by planning a little too much, and then have the team settle down to just the right amount.

person feels taken care of and supported. I let the person know that I expect him or her to focus on doing a great job and to let me know right away if there is anything that he or she needs.

Supporting Self-Management

The more each person takes charge of his or her own work and gets it done right, the more likely the project is to succeed. Also, people are more motivated and enjoy their work more when they figure out how to do a job themselves. So, I don't micromanage. Instead, I *teach* all the tools of planning and management. You might say that I turn each worker into a project manager for his or her part of the project.

Most small business owners find that it is risky to delegate jobs to employees. Most often, we find that the job doesn't get done as well as we ourselves would do it. With the approach in *Project Management for Small Business Made Easy,* you can minimize that difference. If the worker has the HIRAST qualities listed above, then he or she can start on small tasks and work up to larger and larger tasks with clear self-management. If we teach the seven parts of the job, then ask the worker to check those seven parts, we teach the worker to walk through the work, planning ahead and avoiding problems. Sometimes, the worker will take our advice and do things the way we know works. Other times, the worker will learn on his or her own, but we make sure the mistakes are small enough to be affordable. And sometimes, we find the worker is better at the job than we could ever be. That's when we know we have a team.

Creating this friendly, professional, success-oriented environment has another real plus to it. We reduce employee turnover and churn. Employees discover that being treated well is rare—and being trusted is even rarer. Employees stay with bosses who provide support and companies that provide opportunities for professional growth and learning.

Supporting Effective Team Communications

Effective communications is essential to project success. So often, we leave out one small detail and then we have to redo the work. To prevent this, we have to teach our team members to think through details, request what is needed in

Bad news is good news. When we hear bad news, we can fix the problem fast.

detail, and work together to get it done right the first time. Even worse, it is only human to get frustrated, upset, or even angry when things don't go well. If we do this as managers, though, we send a message: *I don't want to hear bad news*. And, of course, we *do* want to hear bad news. The sooner we hear bad news, the sooner we can fix it.

When it comes to communications, we have to lead by example. If we communicate clearly and effectively; if we thank people for telling us what's going on, even when the news is bad; and if we apologize when we make a mistake and get a little snippy, then our team members will be open to learning to do likewise.

When the team is ready to learn, show them Figure 10-2 and explain why both levels of feedback are essential.

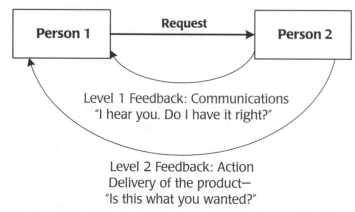

Figure 10-2. The two levels of feedback

Feedback is information that we receive that allows us to correct our course.

Let's say that you want to tell me what to do. After you speak, I repeat back a short version of the instructions. If I got it right, you let me know. If not, you correct my understanding, and we check again. That's level-1 feedback. Now, I know what I've agreed to do. But I still have to do it! Doing the work and then asking, "Is this what you wanted?" is level-2 feedback. Now, either you have what you want or you tell me what I need to do to fix it. If you think of a waiter at a restaurant, level-1 feedback is when he checks to make sure he got your order right and level-2 feedback is when he delivers the food you ordered and makes sure you don't need anything else.

Good customer service is just this: understand the job, do the job, and check that the customer is happy.

When we have a project plan and then all team members make a habit of doing good level-1 and level-2 feedback, something wonderful happens. We get a highly effective process called *customer service within the team*. Remember: our project action plan is essentially linked tasks, with the output of one task being the input for the next task. Now that each task is clearly defined, team members go to the next person in line and say, "My output is your input. If I give you this, will you have everything you need to do a good job easily?" The future recipient of the work defines exactly what he or she is going to need. Then the first person does the work, delivers it, and asks, "Is this all you need?" The recipient checks the work and almost always it's just right. Then that worker gets going. And when he or she does, the focus is on quality. Instead of facing the hassle of running around to find things and fixing inputs, the worker has everything right there and gets to work to deliver excellent results. This goes all the way down the line to the delighted customer at the end of the project.

The workers keep working and we keep everything rolling all the way to success.

As managers, we just grease the wheels and keep them rolling. We make sure that the clearly defined requests that specify outputs are written down and we make sure that all seven elements of each job are available to the workers.

Conclusion: Team Success™

If there is one idea that underlies this whole approach, it is *cooperation*. We work with our team. Our team works with us on the project. And we all work to make sure that the customer gets whatever features will provide the benefits that deliver the highest value. The beauty of this approach is that it's not just a win for the customer and it's not just a win for the company. It's a win for the team, as well. It's what I call *win-win, all the way around*.

Remember the three steps of a project: prepare, do, and follow through? Well, your preparations are almost done. Two more chapters, Chapter 11, Getting What You Need, which talks about purchasing, and Chapter 12, Pulling the Plan Together, will leave you fully prepared for a project that will speed its way to success.

Chapter 11

Getting What You Need

THE FORMAL NAME FOR THE SUBJECT OF THIS CHAPTER IS *PROJECT Procurement Management*. That name is just too fancy. Also, most of what the Project Management Institute teaches about putting out requests for proposals, comparing bids to select vendors, and managing contracts doesn't apply to us small business folks, anyway. So, in Chapter 11, Getting What You Need, I focus on the following issues:

▶ Purchasing for projects

▶ Getting expertise

▶ Getting information

▶ Getting permission

▶ Evaluating vendors

▶ Tracking and saving money in the purchasing process

Although this work is a small part of our project, doing it well is a big prevention of project problems. Everything we need from outside the project—every *external dependency*—is a project risk. So some extra attention is called for to prevent problems.

In fact, I ran across a project procurement problem today, as I was writing this book. I'm working on arranging an event and certain things need to be in place before the event. One of them requires a permit. This is going to create a big delay, because I'm dealing with a company that makes stone monuments that operates out of the stone age. They don't do e-mail. They won't do a contract by fax, because they need original signed copies. So, everything has to go through the mail to three people, which adds a week or two to the project. In this case, if we miss a certain date, the event will be delayed by another four months. So I'm spending time calling people to ask them to be ready to check their mailboxes so that they can sign documents and mail them to other people. If all that works, the whole thing might work out. But I can't be sure, because there's a subcontractor involved and no one will talk to him until all the paperwork is signed.

Poorly planned purchases are project pitfalls.

If I were doing the same work in an industry that used e-mail and accepted faxed signatures, all this work would be done in an afternoon. Instead, all I can do is put it in motion, spend all next week making reminder calls, and keep my fingers crossed. That's what I mean by hassle. In small companies, we project managers spend our time taking care of that stuff, either because there's no one else to do it or because we want our team to get the work done, so we push the hassles out of the way.

Purchasing for Projects

There are a few lessons from the story of the stone monument paperwork:

- The only way to find out all the rules, glitches, and possible delays is to talk with everyone. And even then, someone usually leaves something out.

The moment you are working with someone new, everything gets three times harder.

- Projects are unique, so purchases for projects are often unique. We may be buying something from an industry we've never dealt with before. When we don't know the ropes, we're more likely to make assumptions and mistakes.

- One little delay causes an endless hassle. This is especially true when you're dealing with multiple vendors and permits. Anyone who's tried to buy a piece of property—dealing with owners, real estate agents, mortgage brokers, mortgage lenders, assessors, and inspectors—knows exactly what I'm talking about.

▶ On a project, those hassles and delays add up to missed deadlines. In routine production work, we consider all the hassles to be part of the cost of doing business and live with it. But, in project management, the delays in each step mean lost work time for the team, missed deadlines, and a cascading series of delays that can lead to major loss of value or even failure of the project.

On a project, the cost of the hassle is a lot higher.

Because of these three problems, we have to pay more attention to a purchase for a project than for a routine office purchase. Here are some tips:

▶ Plan and make purchases early. Give yourself plenty of lead time.

▶ Let your vendors know that you are on a project and that getting it done right and getting it on time are crucial to your success.

Can't My Administrative Assistant Handle This?

Project purchasing seems like the ideal job for an administrative assistant. And, after the plan is done, it is. During planning, we need to take the lead, because planning the right purchase often requires talking with several experts and learning a lot. But, when it comes to ordering things and taking care of communications and paperwork, it seems like an administrative assistant would be ideal.

An *ideal* administrative assistant would be ideal. Unfortunately, such a person is—according to most small business owners I talk with—very hard to find. The clear thinking and attention to detail that it takes to talk with others on the phone—people they have never met—and get those people to get the job done right are very rare. Even if the administrative assistant keeps track of everything and calls everyone, he or she may not have what it takes to get others to do what they need to do. Also, workers tend to think that if they get four out of five jobs done, they've done really well. But, on a project, that's like fixing four out of five problems with the car, but forgetting to fill the gas tank. The project won't go anywhere unless every external dependency gets it done right.

So it takes an unusually excellent administrative assistant to do this kind of work. And it takes an unusually courageous project manager or business owner to put the fate of a project in the hands of an assistant. I have managed to train people to the job a couple of times, but it has never been easy.

The Lesson: Something small business owners wish wasn't true, but is all too often, is the adage: *If you want something done right, do it yourself.* We should do our best to get past that and delegate. But we should also realize that project success may require that we keep on top of purchasing details.

▶ Let your vendors guide you. Tell them that their products are new for you, let them advise you, and let them walk you through the steps. In most cases, the ones who are willing to do this are the best people to work with. Informative people are often also reliable.

Getting Expertise

Sometimes, we don't need products or services; we need expertise and knowledge. Usually, this comes in one of two forms: we need either training or guidance. In training, we and our team learn how to do something and then apply the ideas ourselves. In guidance, we and our team receive specific direction on how to prepare for or to do the project.

The big challenge is this: if we're not experts, how can we tell good advice from bad?

It isn't easy. The key is to find people who are genuinely committed to the success of their customers. People who are trying to sell you solutions to make a living for themselves are a hit-or-miss crowd. You might get something good, but you might not. People who are truly dedicated to quality and customer service will let you talk with their customers, so you can get references and referrals. For example, when I needed a new web site, I spent six months looking for a person with the right experience and expertise. I chose him and it totally paid off.

First, read, learn, and look around so that you can ask good questions. Write up a clear description of what you are looking for. A bit of internet research is a great idea. Once you have a good description of what you want to know, call up some trainers or vendors or read their web sites and course descriptions. Or go to the bookstore and browse a bunch of books on the subject. Find one that makes sense for you. Try to get answers to two or three of your questions right off. Look for a book or class that starts at the right level for you and gives you what you need to know. Trust your gut. You'll know it when you find it.

Once you've done this, talk with experts. Tell them what you've learned. The expert you want to work with is the one who will take the time to tell you why you're wrong when you're wrong and steer you the right way. Someone who does that before he or she starts getting paid is already steering you right and will give you good guidance when you hire him or her.

Find vendors who are willing to collaborate, who will make your success their success.

Make your questions clear. Then find an answer that fits your questions.

There is another approach. Accept your own total ignorance and then find someone else who has already used an expert and gotten what he or she wanted. Follow these referrals, check out two or three vendors, and pick one you can work with, who will take you by the hand and lead you every step of the way in a way that you can understand.

When you want to know how to do something, you can ignore people who say, "That's impossible." What they really mean is "I don't know how to do that." If you really want to do something and someone says, "That's impossible," reply, "Thank you for letting me know you don't know how to do it. I'll go find someone who does." Of course, you may not want to say that aloud. But that's how you should be thinking.

Getting Information

There is an amazing amount of information available for free on the internet.

Sometimes, we simply need information. We may just need to know certain facts for a project or we may need to get information as a first step toward finding the right book, the right training class, or the right vendor. The internet is an amazing timesaver here. If you don't know how to do research on the internet, take a few hours and learn—it will save you weeks of time within a year. And most of what you are looking for is available for free.

If we want to succeed, we want good information. But what makes information good? That varies. Here are some key points:

▶ *Correct* information is what we want when we're doing something that involves engineering, involves making things work.

▶ *Authoritative* information comes from an official source; we want to use that if we're going to make an official statement of our own.

▶ Information needs to be *precise* enough to give us the accuracy we need to do our job. For example, if we're just speaking generally, we can say a marathon is a 26-mile run. But if we want to train runners, we need to know that it is 26 miles and 385 yards. (I just looked that up on the internet, at www.wikipedia.org.)

▶ Information needs to be *appropriate*. It has to answer our questions and tell us how to do what we need to do.

▶ Information needs to be *current*. Some information goes out of date all too quickly.

Decide how good your information needs to be. Do you need the official answer (authoritative)? The best, expert answer? Or maybe just an answer that's good enough to get the job done.

When we have good information, our chances of project success go way up.

Getting Permission

Sometimes, we need permission. An obvious case is building permits for a construction project.

But I remember one time when my project ran into trouble because I couldn't get permission to go into a government building. I had completed a project where I built a prototype of a new computer. I was headed for the final meeting where I had to display the computer to a bunch of federal executives. I came to their building. The guards at the front desk wouldn't let me bring the computer into the building. They had a procedure for giving permission to sign out a computer to take it *out* of the building, but they couldn't find any rules for letting a computer *into* the building. Understand, this was a government computer and I was simply bringing it from one government building to another. But there was no way to get it in the door. It took over half an hour to convince them that they didn't have any procedures because there were no rules because it *just didn't matter*. I was half an hour late for my presentation to my client because their guards wouldn't let me in the door.

The lesson is that we have to ask questions. Learn what the rules are. Learn what the problems are. And, when trying to get permission, expect delays as paper is passed around from one person to another. You won't get to talk with these people. They won't know that your project is on the line—

Input-Process-Output Strikes Again

To help get permissions and information, you can use two tools from Chapter 10, Teamwork and Communications. First of all, think of the task of getting one question answered or one permission granted as an input-process-output flow from your question or request through the decision to your receipt of the information or official permission. Second, for each step—input, process, and output—use the two levels of feedback. Find out if they understood your question or request. Find out if they made a decision. Find out if they sent the information or permission. Find out if you received it. Find out if it is what you need. Don't drop the ball and don't let anyone else drop the ball.

and maybe your business, too. If they did, they might care—or they might not. These are the people who care about signatures, who need originals not faxes, who reject a 20-page form because one box isn't checked. So, with permissions more than with anything else, start early, learn the ropes, and keep tracking what is happening.

The challenge with getting permission is often that the person or organization giving permission cares more about not making a mistake than about helping you to succeed. The guard doesn't want to let the wrong person into the building. The town council wants to stop the wrong kind of development. But, some days, it seems that no one really wants to see good work get done. As project managers, the best we can do is to talk with these people and let them know three things:

▶ We care about their concerns.

▶ We will follow all of their steps and rules.

▶ They can really help us a lot by moving us through their process quickly.

If we do that, things will go as well as they can. So, if we identify permission requirements early and allow enough time in our schedule for some delay, we should be able to make it work.

Evaluating Vendors

The bigger the project, the more important it is to evaluate vendors carefully. We need to look at vendors for products and short-term services in one way and vendors for long-term services differently.

Vendors for Products and Short-Term Services

If we are buying a product or piece of equipment for our project, here are the most important considerations in choosing vendor and product:

▶ The vendor understands the business and technical requirements and can guide us in product selection and confirm that the product we are choosing is suited to the task.

▶ The vendor is highly reliable and will deliver on time.

▶ Any payment, contract, or purchasing requirements are upfront, clear, and reasonable.

▶ The vendor provides good after-purchase customer support and technical support to help us through any problems in installing and using the product.

The same considerations apply to short-term services, such as delivery services, catering, and so forth. We should pay attention to these issues, discuss them with our vendors, and search for evidence of good business practices, such as referrals, references, and reports from the Better Business Bureau, the Chamber of Commerce, and professional associations.

*P*roject success requires good products from good vendors.

Bent Package, Bad Day

TV production has some strange requirements. A colleague of mine, Matt Williams, produces TV commercials. One time, he was doing a shoot of some medicine bottles on a table. The labels had been specially printed for quality and alignment so they would look good on TV. They were delivered by messenger. Unfortunately, the messenger was not familiar with the requirements of TV production and he allowed the package and the labels to be bent on their way across town.

Matt had to rearrange the morning shooting schedule while waiting for a courier to run around town getting replacement labels, these ones packed in a solid box. With TV production time costing over $1,000 per hour, this slight shipping slip-up could have been very expensive.

The Lesson: Your vendors don't know your needs. Make sure they do.

Vendors for Long-Term Services

Sometimes, we want to use someone from outside our company for most or all of the length of the project. In this case, we need to do a deeper evaluation and check the vendors against our requirements more rigorously. This applies whether we are hiring a consultant to join (or even lead) the team or we are outsourcing the project entirely to a consulting firm or vendor. In your business, you may already use subcontractors routinely. If you do, these issues will be familiar to you. But if you don't and you need to hire contract labor or a contractor's team for a project, then this topic is worth studying as you launch the project. And, if you are familiar with contracting in your own industry, but now need services from a different industry, watch your assumptions. The rules are likely to be different.

The key issue is that we must make sure that the contractor's goals and our own goals are aligned all the way through the project. This includes:

▶ Making sure the contractor is committed for the length of the project. If you hire someone who will leave for a better opportunity, that is a big project risk.

▶ Making sure the contractor is available for the length of the project.

▶ Making sure that the contractor understands and is committed to all project requirements.

▶ Creating incentives and pay schedules that keep the benefits for the contractor in line with your goals.

▶ Creating good communications that hold true throughout the project and include enough detail so that there are no surprises.

The most important single factor in vendor selection should be lots of proven experience doing work a lot like your project for customers a lot like you.

A good contractor can actually guide you through this process. Unfortunately, there are also those who talk a good talk, but don't walk their talk when the time comes. You are offering a lot when you offer a project contract and you should require a lot as well. Auditors have a saying: "Trust, and verify." In this case, this means that you give vendors the benefit of the doubt, but then you also talk with prior clients and check the background of the companies and people you will be working with. Gut instinct plus conversation plus checking are essential in vendor selection.

A good contractor has to join your team to work well with you. Expertise is essential, but compatibility is also crucial. Make sure the vendor can work with you and your team.

If at all possible, check out at least two or three vendors. More is even better. It may be clear that one comes out on top, but, if so, you should be able to say why. The number of years of experience? The type of experience? The glowing reports from satisfied clients? The recommendation of someone you really trust? Know why you are making your choice and, if your choice is based on price alone, know that you are risking your money and your project to maybe save a few dollars.

Tracking and Saving Money in the Purchasing Process

So far, our focus has been on quality. There's a good reason for this. Saving a percentage of total cost but getting products or vendors who don't perform ends up costing us a lot more than paying a premium for quality products and service. In fact, the biggest cost may be that the project fails altogether.

Even so, cost matters. We should set up a system for tracking costs as we go and saving money where cost savings don't compromise quality and don't add risk to the project. Here are some ways to do that.

- ▶ Set up a separate accounting system for your project. This can be a subset of your regular accounting program or it can be a separate tracking system using a spreadsheet.

- ▶ Require weekly accounting for hours and frequent billing.

- ▶ Arrange for payment on your approval of deliverables throughout the project. Make sure the work is done right before you pay.

- ▶ Be aware of and track all types of cost, including
  - External costs that you pay as expenses.
  - Internal costs that you pay as salary.
  - Other internal costs, such as supplies used up by the project that could be used for something else.
  - Costs you may not usually track, such as the use of office space or equipment time that, if not used for the project, could be used for something else.

Regarding routine supplies and equipment time, don't be caught short. Perhaps you're generally using up a certain amount of colored paper each month at your photocopier. When you launch a special marketing project that includes fliers, be sure to order extra paper and bill it to the project. Then you'll run into trouble only when you run out of toner. So order that, too!

Conclusion: Hassle-Free and Good to Go!

For most projects, purchasing simply requires early planning, allowing some leeway for external resources who will often run late or make mistakes, and keeping on top of those external resources and vendors to minimize hassle. Sometimes, we need to make extra effort to research new topics, get training, or evaluate vendors for products, short-term services, or subcontracting for larger parts of the project. At the beginning of each project, evaluate what your needs are likely to be. Then review this chapter and follow these tips to success.

Congratulations—you've planned every dimension of your project. Now you're ready for the last step of preparation, which you'll learn how to do in Chapter 12, Pulling the Plan Together.

Chapter 12

Pulling the Plan Together

W E'VE NOW PLANNED EVERY ASPECT OF OUR PROJECT, DONE A lot of preparation, and learned how to prevent a whole lot of problems and bring a whole lot of issues and difficult situations under control. Let's pull all this together by taking care of these final items:

▶ *Tying the plan together.* We'll look at how the nine knowledge areas work together to make a single plan.

▶ *What if the plan changes?* If it does, we'll be ready with *integrated change management*.

▶ *The preparation review gate* is our final check before we launch the *doing stage* of the project.

When you've taken these steps, you'll be fully prepared and ready to do the project and steer it to success!

Tying the Plan Together

In working up the project plan, we've looked at eight areas of project management: scope, time, cost, quality, risk, human resources, communications, and procurement. With eight perspectives, it can be hard to see that, all together, they make one plan. Let's see how the eight areas work together and then learn about the ninth area—*project integration management*. Using the ninth area, we'll have one solid plan, good to go.

In organizing the nine areas of project management we'll distinguish three that lead to defined, measurable results (r) and six that support these results, but that are measured by tracking our process (p). We'll start with the three (r) results areas, which are related to one another by what is called the *iron triangle*.

The Iron Triangle: Scope, Time, and Cost

Iron doesn't bend or stretch. And there's a rule about triangles: if you change the length of one side, you have to change the length of one of the other sides to keep the shape of the triangle. The *iron triangle* illustrates a rule in project management: you can't deliver more on a project (increase scope), without spending more and taking longer (increasing time and cost). This is illustrated in Figure 12-1, the iron triangle.

The main use of this tool is to educate customers and executives on the fact that, if they ask for more results, you're going to ask for more time and money.

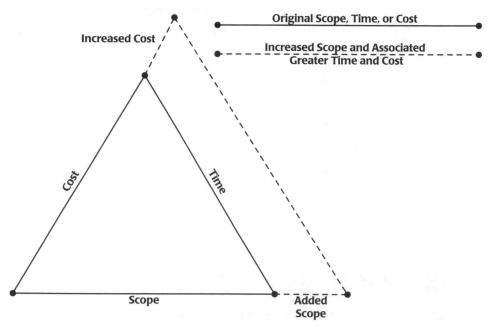

Figure 12-1. The *iron triangle* of scope, time, and cost

The goal is to prevent *scope creep*, which is the addition of more and more items to the project, until the project is so stuffed with stuff to do that we can no more move ahead than we can run a marathon after a Thanksgiving dinner. When people understand scope creep, they know that the answer to the question, "Can you do this, too?" is "Maybe, but it's going to cost you and it will delay the project."

I said, "Maybe" for two reasons.

The 1:10:100 rule we introduced in Chapter 3, Prepare, Do, Follow Through, is crucial here. Anything added after the end of preparation will take ten times longer and cost ten times more to do in this project than it will cost if we wait until later and do it as a little project on its own. The *preparation review gate*—the subject of this chapter—is our last chance to put in whatever should go into the project and leave out whatever should be left out.

The second reason I said, "Maybe" has to do with risk. Every added goal adds risk. Every change to the plan adds more risk. We have to refuse some changes to our project plan because trying to do that one more thing risks causing the whole project to run into big, big trouble.

The iron triangle also reminds us of the three main measures of project success:

▶ Deliver the right results

▶ On time

▶ Within our budget

Bringing the other six areas of project management under control helps make sure we succeed in achieving our basic goal. Let's review now the five areas that we've discussed so far.

P roject results: deliver the requested product with quality on time and within budget.

Supporting Success: Quality, Risk, Human Resources, Communications, and Procurement

As we saw in Chapters 8, 9, 10, and 11, these five areas of project management help us bring everything that matters to the project under management. Through these management processes (p), we are able to ensure and improve upon the basic results (r) of delivering our scope on time and within budget. Table 12-1 illustrates how these five additional areas support the core three goals of the iron triangle. (It also shows the last area, *integration*, which we'll discuss later.)

Area	Question(s)	Issue(s) Brought Under Management
The Iron Triangle—Results (r)		
Scope	*Why* are we doing this project? *What* are we making? *How* will we make it?	Definition of project results
Time	*When* will we do it?	Effort and duration, time estimate
Cost	*How much* time will it take? How *much* money will it cost?	Cost, budget, and cost estimation
Supporting Knowledge Areas—Process (p)		
Quality	*What makes it good?*	Errors in design Errors in process
Risk	*How can we make sure* it gets done? *What could go wrong?*	Uncertainty—the fact we can't know the future
Human Resources	*Who* will do it?	Getting the right people and giving them the right skills
Communications	*How will we keep in touch and stay on the same page?*	Mutual understanding
Procurement	*What do we need* and *how will we get it?*	Acquisition of products and services from external sources
Integration	*How do we keep it all together?* *Whether* we should do the project or cancel it?	The links between one area and another Project change

Table 12-1. Project management areas, questions, and issues

If you've done all the work recommended up to now in *Project Management for Small Business Made Easy*, then you've covered all the areas except project integration management, which we will cover in this chapter. You know everything there is to know about your project. If your project is a sailing trip, then you've got your plan and destination, all your supplies are on board, your crew is ready, and you're ready to do the final checks you need to do before you set sail.

Integration

In project integration management, we deal with four issues:

- ▶ How do changes in one area of the project affect the rest of the project?
- ▶ What if the plan changes or needs to change?
- ▶ How do we keep track of what's going on and keep the project moving?
- ▶ What if we need to think about canceling the project?

Let's look at the first question: How do changes in one area of the project affect the rest of the project? Let's use our example of a sailing ship. If getting supplies goes out of control, then we depart late and the whole project might run late. If the size of our cargo is out of control, people could keep throwing more on until too much is loaded and the whole ship could sink. That would be like scope creep causing project failure.

The point is that if any one of the nine areas goes in an unexpected direction, we have to bring that back under control. Otherwise, we're in uncharted territory, off our map, and the whole project could go out of control.

Catch problems early, before they cascade into disaster.

This is why the process (p) areas, the ones that are hard to measure, the ones that don't have an easily definable single result, are so essential to the success of the project results, the (r) factors. Procurement, communications, quality, risk, and human resources (teamwork) are all essential to ensure scope, time, and quality. Once we understand how important that is, we don't hesitate to plan for all nine areas on every project. Once we plan it all, we'll have to keep everything under management throughout the project, and that is the subject of Chapter 13, Keeping Everything on Track.

Right now, we'll look at what to do if the plan changes and how we decide if we should go ahead with the project or cancel it, using review gates.

What if the Plan Changes?

We've completed our plan. But what if the plan changes, or someone wants it to change, or it needs to change? As we've already noted, because of the 1:10:100 rule, any changes after the preparation stage will be very expensive. So we need to be ready for the possibility of change. In particular, we need to be ready with a clear process for keeping these situations under control:

- ▶ Someone on the project wants a change.

- ▶ The project gets changed before you hear about it.

- ▶ There is a real need to change the project, either because of a big error in the original plan or because reality has changed and what we are planning to do won't work or won't be valuable to the customer any more.

We can think about each suggestion or request for a change to the project as a project *change request*. We handle change requests by creating an *integrated change management system* that:

- ▶ Has a standard form and a standard process for handling every change request.

- ▶ Ensures that everyone on the project knows that all ideas about changes and all change requests must come to you as the project manager.

- ▶ Gives you clear criteria for deciding whether to change the project or not.

Things change. Manage that change proactively.

In general, if we have educated all team members and the customer about the 1:10:100 rule and how good planning keeps costs down, then we should run into relatively few change requests. Still, if people do want change, it's your job to know that they're thinking about it, to hear the ideas and reasons and get them written down early, and to bring the change request under management.

Changes are rare in short, routine projects. The longer the project, the more people involved, and the more rapidly changing the field in which the project is working, the more likely that there will be a need for project change. Also, some situations are simply harder to investigate during planning. Then, when we encounter something unknown, we have to find out what is happening and change the project to take care of the problem. Here are two examples of that:

- ▶ The town I'm living in spent a year fixing old sewer pipes. Most of the fixes were done by pumping chemicals through the system to coat the pipes. But, when there was a lot of decay or leaks showed up, they had to dig into the ground and replace the pipes. They knew that pipe replacement would be necessary, but they couldn't know how much or where it would be needed until they were doing the work.

▶ A State Police agency needed to make changes to software that had been written 30 years earlier and patched and modified through the years without any records of those changes. Figuring out how to bring that system up to date was a lot like trying to fix underground pipes. Even though we could see the computer code, no one could figure out how it worked.

In general, building something new has fewer problems related to unexpected situations than trying to renovate something old. The Pentagon—the building that holds the center of the United States Department of Defense—was build from the ground up in 17 months. It will take 17 years to renovate the building, because the workers have to clean out the old problems before putting in new insulation, electric wiring, and everything else and because people are working in the building while they're trying to fix it.

Computer professionals have a reminder about these problems: before you drain the swamp, be sure to get the alligators out. But the only way to get alligators out of a swamp is to drain it. And it's really hard to know what to do when you're up to your neck in alligators.

To keep changes to the project plan under control:

▶ Educate everyone about the cost of change and the necessity to get all ideas about change to you.

▶ Create forms and a process for managing change requests or download mine from www.qualitytechnology.com/DoneRight.

▶ Write down every change request.

▶ Evaluate each change request promptly.

▶ Make the change only if one of the following is true:
  – The project just won't work without the change.
  – The project will fail without the change.
  – It's still pretty early in the *doing stage* of the project, the change is small, and it will improve things a lot without compromising quality or adding risk.

Now, your plan is complete and you're ready to change it if you have to. It's time for the final review of your preparations.

The Preparation Review Gate

*A*ny error still in the plan now will cost ten times more to fix later.

If you've been building a project plan while reading this book, you're ready for the final review of the plan before declaring the plan ready, confirming you're prepared, and launching the *doing stage* of the project. If this is a one-person project, just read the plan over and you're ready for the review. If the plan has been prepared by a team, then have each member read over the plan and then ask everyone, "Is there anything we've left out? Is there anything we thought of, but never wrote down? Is this exactly what you plan to do?" When everyone agrees on the plan, the plan and preparations are ready for review.

Review is a process, which means it has an input and an output:

▶ *The input* is the plan plus all the preparations to date.

▶ *The process* is reading, questioning, checking details, and cross-checking parts of the plan.

▶ *The output* is one of these four things:
  – *Approval* that the plan is complete and all preparations are ready, so that the *doing stage* is launched.
  – *Provisional approval* pending small changes. Here, the statement is "Take care of this list of things, make sure they're done right, and then go ahead."
  – *Required rework* of all or part of the plan, followed by a second *preparation gate review*. We do this if big changes are needed to the plan and those changes will take some time. For example, if we discover in the review that the project result isn't what the customer wants or that some major element of the project is unworkable or too risky, we call for rework and a second review.
  – *Project cancellation* if we discover the plan just isn't doable or isn't worth doing.

*E*ach end-of-stage review is a safety net. By taking the possibility of cancellation seriously, we save the company from wasting time and money on something that won't work.

Of course, we hope for success. But our review should be independent and should ask, "What's best for the company?" Don't say, "But we've already put in so much time, we should go ahead." Time and money spent are *sunk cost* and should not be considered when deciding what to do next. Even if we do find a major problem, we don't dive into doom and gloom. If we can, we fix the problem. If not, we appreciate the fact that we've just protected the company from a big mistake, we learn our lesson, and we set a new direction.

Put Preferences Aside and Make Sure Your Project Is Safe to Go

Of course, we hope that the plan is good and it can go ahead with few or no changes. And every trapeze artist hopes to catch the trapeze at the other end. But most trapeze artists perform with a safety net anyway. The review is our safety net—don't cut it out from under yourself by pushing through a plan with a problem. Go ahead only if the project is safe and sure.

The Lesson: Review your project as if you're preparing for a circus stunt. Your safety and that of your team may not actually be on the line, but your time and money are—and maybe your company, too.

Running the Review

The two biggest things to look for in the preparation stage review are assumptions and misunderstandings:

▶ *Assumptions* are dangerous because, if an assumption is wrong, the project is going to get into trouble. Behind most big problems, there's someone saying, "I assumed …." Every assumption in our plan should be identified, written down, and verified during planning and preparation. If it hasn't been, then it should become a work item required by the review team. If an assumption cannot be verified—if, for example, it's a possible alligator in the swamp—then it should be included as a risk item on our risk list and kept under management.

▶ *Misunderstandings* cause people to have different ideas about what we are making on a project, in spite of all our planning and communications. Include everyone on the team and key customers in the review. Then make sure that everyone sees things the same way. If not, identify the differences. If the misunderstandings can be resolved easily, then write down the clarification and agreement and move ahead with the updated plan. If not, then make time for rework and, if necessary, consider project cancellation.

Eliminate assumptions and misunderstandings.

Let's take a closer look at the review process steps mentioned above:

▶ *Reading.* Everyone on the team should read the whole plan before the review meeting, highlight any questionable items, and note any concerns.

- ▶ *Questioning.* Here are some good questions to ask:
    - − Are all 14 questions from Table 12-1 answered?
    - − Does every part of the plan meet the requirements for a good specification listed in Chapter 6, What Are We Making?
    - − Does everyone agree on what each key goal actually looks like?
- ▶ *Checking details.* Here, we check facts, question assumptions, and check the math on our calculations. One excellent tool for checking details is a *walk-through,* where we read through the plan together and imagine doing each step of the process. This is what Hollywood moviemakers do with their scripts to make sure everyone is literally on the same page and every detail is good to go.
- ▶ *Cross-checking parts of the plan.* Is every item listed in the scope also in the schedule and in the budget? Are all items and services to be purchased listed in the procurement plan? Was every item included when preparing the quality and risk plans and is every person included in the communications plan? In a good project plan, each of the plans from the different areas of project management knowledge is a different facet looking into the same gem. We have eight angles, but, if the plan is not flawed, we have eight views of the same reality—our project as we will do it.

Revision and Final Preparation

If the plan passes all of these tests, we're good to go. If there are small changes, make them and check to make sure they are right. A project can get into a real mess if an issue is raised during a review, but not resolved in writing. Some people will end up making one thing and others doing something else. When a project team works like that, you get the head of a horse and the back end of a donkey—and you end up looking like a horse's rear end.

Remember that review is a process and that the rework and follow-up review are processes, as well. Processes take time and effort. Put the review processes and rework time for each gate into your budget. Then do the review, do all the rework, and run a second review if you have to. When you've done that, you have a bulletproof project.

Conclusion: Set Sail!

We're more than halfway through this book and, if you've been preparing a project plan as you go, your project is already past the worst dangers. That's right: most projects that fail or go way over budget or hit big delays made big mistakes in planning or just didn't plan everything that could have been planned. If you've written a project plan using everything you've learned so far in *Project Management for Small Business Made Easy,* you're way ahead of the curve and very likely to succeed.

When a ship has a destination, a course laid in, a cargo loaded, and all preparations complete and checked, it's time to pull away from the dock. We set sail on a project by declaring the preparation stage complete and launching the *doing stage.* And, just like in sailing, the key to project success is to keep the project afloat, keep moving in the right direction, correct the course when necessary, and keep an eye out for storms and sea monsters. You'll learn how to do that in Chapter 13, Keeping Everything on Track. Let's sail on!

Chapter 13

Keeping Everything on Track

THIS CHAPTER HAS THREE SIMPLE PURPOSES. *O*NE IS TO TEACH YOU how to run a project status meeting. Another is to give you the concept of receiving status information, generating a status report, and then planning and taking corrective action to keep the project on track. Once you've done those two things, you are ready for the third: to manage the *doing stage* of your project, keeping everything under control until you deliver the product on time and under budget. We'll look at how to do this by discussing practical course correction.

The Status Meeting

Status is for a project what location is for a sailboat. Status measures scope—what we've gotten done—against effort spent and money spent. A status meeting is a process that includes determining status, deciding what to do, and initiating any new actions.

The status meeting process begins before the actual meeting, when we gather information from team members about what work has been done and about how much time and money has been spent. If we were sailing, we

116

would get our location, plot it on a map, and then call in the crew to decide how to change course. The same is true in a status meeting—we get the information before the meeting, figure out what the issues are, and then call the meeting to decide what to do next.

When we receive status information, the news may be good or bad. It doesn't matter. The first thing we should do is say, "Thank you for letting me know." Then stop, breathe, and make sure that the team member really heard you. Only after that do you say something between "Great! I'm glad you got all that done" and "Oh, my! We'll have to figure out how to fix that."

There is only one right way to receive a status report—by saying, "Thank you!"

Figure 13-1 shows how work done, time, cost, and risk relate to a sailing trip.

The location of our sailboat is status information. On a project, the equivalent is the answers to these questions:

▶ What work have we got done?

▶ How many hours of effort and days of duration have we used?

▶ How much money have we spent?

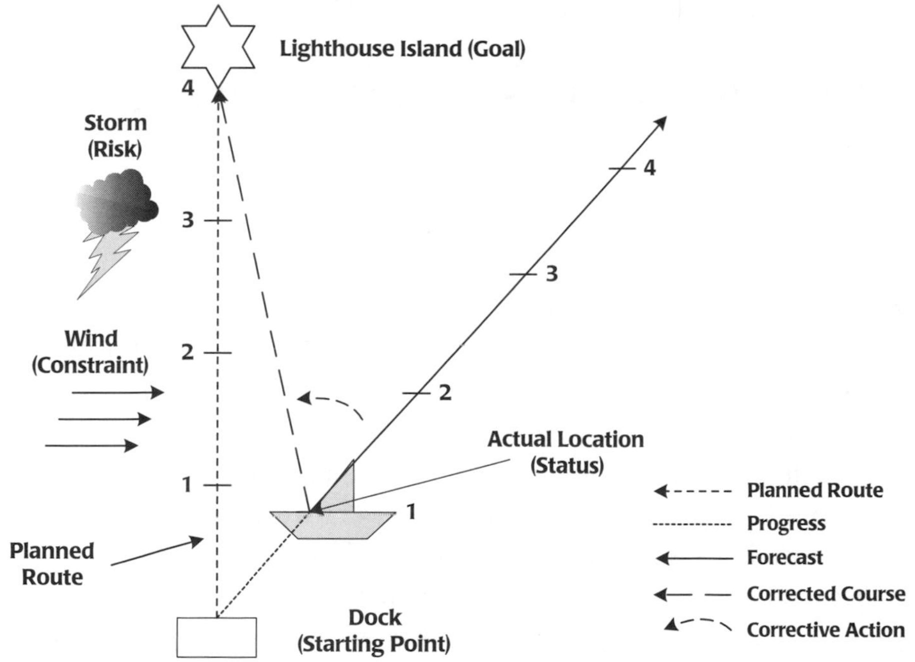

Figure 13-1. Status of a sailing trip

When we plot the answers to those questions against our plan, we're comparing our actual work results, effort, and expenses against our plan. That's like putting the location of the sailboat on the chart that shows our planned route, as in Figure 13-1. The distance from the starting point to where we are now—the work we've done—is our progress. The long diagonal line is a forecast of where we will end up if we don't correct our course. Instead, we plan to correct our course (curved arrow) to reach our destination. By including wind (constraints) and storm (risk), our status meeting can include project risk management as well as scope, time, and cost. We can also ask our team members how they feel about the quality of the work being done and about hassles in the process, so that we check the status of quality. We can check in about communications, teamwork, and purchasing, as well. It is good to touch base on all nine areas of project management each week.

In planning how to correct our course, we integrate all this information and find the best way to get the project done right, focusing most on new things we need to do to prevent or fix project problems and on the work of the upcoming week. We'll look at that in detail at the end of the chapter, after we discuss feedback and control.

The Feedback-and-Control Concept

Feedback backfires when blame and personality get in the way.

Feedback is possibly the most misunderstood management concept. Let's begin by clarifying three key points about the relationship between feedback and criticism.

▶ *Feedback has nothing to do with criticism.* In fact, any kind of criticism, blame, or personality interferes with the good relationships and clear communication essential to effective feedback.

▶ *Negative feedback is course correction.* Negative feedback is not bad. If I tell you, "You're doing a great job. In fact, this is far better than we need. You could ease up on quality and work a little faster, and that would be great for the customer and the project," then that's negative feedback, because it is information that corrects your course.

▶ *Positive feedback is not vague rah-rah.* Positive feedback in business is a very specific message, saying, "Good job! Do it again."

When someone is on course, say, "Good job! Do it again." When someone needs to change direction, appreciate his or her work and give a bit of negative feedback, course correction. If we do this each week, the team does the right work until the project is done.

Negative feedback is course correction. Positive feedback says, "Good job, do it again."

Feedback and Plan, Do, Check, Act (PDCA)

Although the idea of feedback and the Plan, Do, Check, Act (PDCA) method were developed separately, they are very similar. Both involve getting information about where we are, deciding what to do, and then taking corrective action. PDCA was developed by Walter A. Shewhart, a physicist at Bell Labs who developed tools for engineering and business based on scientific principles. (We'll discuss PDCA in Chapter 16, Quality: Eliminate Error.) Feedback was defined by Gregory Bateson, a philosopher and scientist who made important contributions to many fields, including psychology, sociology, the invention of the computer, radar-controlled gunnery, and business management.

The Lesson: Whatever we call it, checking in with reality and correcting our course make good business sense.

Practical Course Correction

In this section, we look at two issues: effective management of the project in the *doing stage* and the eight levels of course correction and change control.

Effective Management of the *Doing Stage*

To implement the status-reporting and course-correction techniques in this chapter effectively, remember these key points:

▶ *Maintain an effective, goal-oriented team environment* with lots of communication and lots of appreciation for good work. This is an effective context for course correction.

▶ *Track reality.* Gather information about work done (scope), time and money spent, risk, quality, and other issues every week, before the status meeting.

▶ *Prepare by plotting your course.* Compare the information with your project plan, action plan, and risk plan before the status meeting. Know whether you are getting enough done. Know what the current risks are. Know what's up on any other issues. Get a sense of your new direction.

Done Is Done

In Chapter 6, What Are We Making? we discussed the importance of clear, precise scope definition, all the way down to the details of work packages and items on our action plan. This pays off now, as we are managing work progress. With small, clear action items, there is no ambiguity. Work is either done or not. No one can say, "It's a big job and I'm partway through."

Let team members know that work counts as done only when it is done, tested, and fixed. We mark a task as done only when the person who is going to use the output as an input for the next task says, "It's good; I can use it." Otherwise, the project will run into trouble. Many projects falter because sloppy definition of work packages lets people say, "I'm working on it; it will be all right." We can't know if that's true, so their work is no longer under management. Then they run late or the work isn't good and it's too late to correct course. This is a major source of project delays.

The Lesson: Define work packages clearly and declare something done only if it's done and it works.

▶ *Plan course correction with your team* in the status meeting.

▶ *Be clear and specific.* Point by point, say either, "Good work! Do it again," or "You're doing well, but I need you to make this change." Be clear. For example, there is a difference between saying, "I need you to get more done by staying focused. Keep the quality right where it is and work faster with more attention," and saying, "I need you to get done. You're paying too much attention to quality beyond what the customer needs. Focus a little less on perfecting the details and more on delivering the work."

Catch small, repeating problems before they sink your project.

The Eight Levels of Course Correction and Change Management

There are four levels of course correction that apply to a project in a routine way, when we are still getting work done according to the original plan:

▶ *Making single small adjustments.* If someone who usually does good work makes a mistake or is running behind, just let him or her know.

▶ *Correcting small repeating problems.* This is probably the biggest risk to a small business project. If things are late or of low quality over and over, there is some underlying cause. Perhaps the person responsible for the task is always being interrupted or doesn't understand the work or have the right skill. Get to the bottom of this and correct it early or the repeated small delays and problems will add up to a very big mess.

▶ *Fixing a major problem.* If one big mistake is made, we need to fix it while keeping the rest of the project moving. Or, on a one-person project, stop, fix the problem, and get back on track. If we've done our risk planning well, we've left leeway in our schedule and budget for one or two problems on a small project and a few on a big one. If not, we'll have to consider project change management (below).

▶ *Dealing with a risk event.* If a risk event happens, we need to both take care of it and also keep the project going. Our advance risk planning will help, but now we need to move into action. On a team project, consider whether you should run the project and let someone else take care of the risk event, or whether you should let someone else guide the project while you take care of the risk event.

Sometimes, we can't follow the original plan, because of an error in the plan or a big change or several risk events. When we change the plan, it is called *rebaselining*. This means that we are working to a new plan, with a new schedule, a new budget, and some new risks as well. Here are the four levels of change management and risk management to deal with these situations:

When project success requires a change to the plan, be clear and decisive.

▶ *Add to the scope.* If, when we evaluate a change request, we decide to add to project scope, we're adding time, cost, and risk. If it is essential so that project results actually add value, then we do it. If it is very beneficial and early enough in the project to make the change, then we might do it. But, in either case, it is equivalent to changing the destination on our sailing trip. We're going to need more time and more food and water (money). Worse, we're going to be sailing into uncharted waters, going to places where we didn't plan to go with unexpected risks.

▶ *Drop something from the scope.* Sometimes we run into trouble—either a big risk event or just a discovery that work can't go as fast as we'd hoped. Then we can't deliver everything on time and within the budget. If we cannot delay delivery and get more money, then we should intentionally drop some part of our scope. This is equivalent to sailing to a closer island, but still making a safe journey. If we don't make this clear, intentional change to the plan, then the rule of the iron triangle will get us. Either we will either run late and over budget anyway or we will drop something, but in an unplanned way or we will simply not finish testing and deliver the result full of errors. Any of those is worse than a clear, planned decision to cut our losses and do a good, well-planned job with the resources available.

▶ *Add more time and/or money.* If we run into trouble—either with a big risk event or with the discovery that our plan left something out or just estimated over-optimistically, we may be able to meet our original project goals by spending more time and/or increasing our budget. If we can extend the deadline with the same team, that usually works. Asking people for overtime or adding people to the team often makes things worse, not better. If we think we can do that, then we should replan the whole project from where we are now to the end and then ask if it is really doable.

▶ *Reevaluate the plan.* Sometimes, major changes to the company or project or a realization that something was wrong at the start force us to reevaluate the whole project plan. We might be considering project cancellation or we might just be saying, "We've got to figure out what's wrong here and fix it." This is called a *project review.* You can learn more about how to do a project review at www.qualitytechnology.com/DoneRight.

Measuring Progress

In *Project Management for Small Business Made Easy,* we've given you the basic tool of work management—managing work done against time and effort, while considering risk and other factors. There is actually a mathematical tool called Earned Value Analysis (EVA) that lets you calculate work done against time and cost and then forecast new completion dates. You can learn about it from the Project Management Institute. For more information, go to my web site, www.qualitytechnology.com/DoneRight.

Conclusion: Steady as She Goes!

In this chapter, you've learned all you need to know to get status information, evaluate status, plan effective corrective action, and put that action into place. Your project should be humming along. In the next five chapters, you'll learn more techniques for managing the project during the *doing stage:*

Course correction can be applied to each area of project management.

- ▶ In Chapter 14, you'll learn to prevent that deadly disease, scope creep.

- ▶ In Chapter 15, you'll learn about how to manage time, money, and purchasing.

- ▶ In Chapter 16, you'll learn lots of good quality management techniques to eliminate errors and ensure that your project results are valuable for—and valued by—both your company and your customers.

- ▶ In Chapter 17, you'll learn about how to keep risk under control throughout the project.

- ▶ In Chapter 18, you'll learn the fine art of managing expectations.

Chapter 14

Prevent Scope Creep

SCOPE CREEP—THE ADDITION OF NEW PIECES TO THE PROJECT AFTER THE plan is done—is a major cause of delivery delays, cost overruns, and project failure. Why does it happen? How do we prevent it?

In this chapter, we'll look at sources of scope creep and ways to manage it. We'll also talk about a related topic—how to know how much to include in a project from the beginning.

Sources of Scope Creep

Scope creep is simply a term for accumulated changes. If we don't have a clearly written plan, then our project plan is like a workshop with lots of doors. Anyone wandering by with a problem or an opportunity can just throw it in and expect us to take care of it for them, for free, as part of our project. If we don't want to be overwhelmed with work, we need to open the door of our project workroom, accept a few jobs, and then shut the door and get to work. Even then, people can ask for changes: "While you're working on the carburetor, could you also check out the transmission?" It is reasonable for people to want everything fixed. It is also reasonable to tell people, "Let's do one thing at a time."

Let's look specifically at why people ask for more and who is most likely to do it.

Why People Ask for More

Good news! Most of the reasons people ask for more are a result of our own poor planning and communications. Why is that news good? Because it means that, if we plan and communicate well, we can prevent most scope creep. Here are common reasons people ask for more and how we can prevent them.

Do what you plan to do and don't do more.

▶ *People weren't included in the original planning.* Find everyone affected by your project and talk with each of them all early.

▶ *People don't understand that requests have to come early.* Educate everyone about the 1:10:100 rule and let everyone know when the gate at the end of planning and preparation is scheduled. Let them know that they have a deadline.

▶ *We don't look closely enough at the initial situation of the project.* This is the "alligators in the swamp" problem we talked about in Chapter 12, Pulling the Plan Together. It happens mostly on projects that are fixing or repairing things. Investigate the current condition of what you are going to fix before you fix it. You might even consider doing two projects. The first would just evaluate the condition of the item or system and then, after the evaluation project is complete, the second would be to make the necessary repairs.

▶ *People don't speak up.* People want something related to the project, but they just keep mum. The best we can do is to encourage people to dream, to define opportunities, and to name problems they want solved and hassles they want to go away. If we encourage regular, truthful, and positive communication about our business, then we can prioritize our projects and include all important work during project planning.

▶ *People get bright ideas.* Here, we encourage brainstorming during planning, so that bright ideas are found early.

▶ *We discover a misunderstanding.* Sometimes, in spite of our best efforts, we don't understand what the customers want during planning. When they see the product, during the *doing stage* or, unfortunately, sometimes at the end of the project, they say, "This isn't what

125

Closet Cleaning out of Control

A student in one of my project management classes told me this story about a weekend project. He offered to clean out and organize a closet for a friend. She agreed and said she would appreciate it as long as it was all done by the time she got back on Sunday afternoon. He got to work Saturday morning. When he emptied the closet, he found a hole in the back wall. He decided to patch the hole. That meant a trip to Home Depot®, where he also decided to buy some racks to use in organizing the closet's contents.

Predictably, Sunday afternoon when his friend returned, he was up to his arms in plaster, his friend's room was full of stuff from the closet, and she was one very unhappy customer.

What went wrong? Several things, all of which you can learn to avoid in this chapter.

> ▶ *Alligator in the swamp.* The hole in the closet wall would have been hard to find before the start of the project. But, on finding it, the helpful student could have put a board in front of it, organized the closet, and let his friend know about the hole.
>
> ▶ *Different priorities.* The closet cleaner wanted to do the job right and do necessary repair work. The customer wanted done what could be done by Sunday afternoon and no more. So, he had a driver toward larger scope and better quality and she had a driver toward less time.
>
> ▶ *Putting his own goals before the customer's.* If the student had stopped to think about what mattered to his friend, he wouldn't have let a closet-cleaning project become a closet-repair project.

The Lesson: Work to the plan and don't feel you have to take care of everything that comes up. Focus on meeting customer goals, not on doing everything you think should be done.

I wanted! Where's my ...?" We can try to prevent this by working in words and pictures, creating a model of what we are doing, or showing the customer a sample of the results we want. Also, be sure to get the customer to approve your plan at the end of planning and preparation and make sure they check the details.

Even if we do a good job preventing all of the causes of scope creep above, change requests will still come in. Here are reasons for change requests that come in spite of our best communications and planning and what we can do about them.

A change outside the project. Our ultimate goal is that project results will provide value to the customer. But what if the customer's situation changes during the project?

Suppose you are renovating a couple's house to make it their dream home and they decide to get a divorce before you finish. Now, they want you to renovate the house for sale to someone else—and that means no pink bathroom with pussycat wallpaper. In a case like this, you need to reinvent the project midstream. Either stop the project or reschedule so that you're doing only work that you're sure is still wanted. Then define the new scope and create a full project plan for all the work that is now needed. If you are changing just a couple of work packages, it's not a big deal. So put in the amount of time needed to make sure that the new project is doable and is planned well. Then launch the project in a new direction.

An alligator in the swamp. In spite of our best efforts, we find something we did not expect about the initial situation of the project. The possibility may or may not be in our risk plan. In either case, we treat it like a risk event. We define the gap between what we expected and what we found. Then we determine the best way to close that gap in line with project goals.

A bright idea. Sometimes, a worker or a customer comes up with an idea that really is an improvement. If it is an easier way of doing what we were planning to do, we should assess the idea for quality and risk and include it if it benefits the project and is safe to do. If it is an enhancement, but a really valuable one, and we are still early in the *doing stage,* we can consider including it. However, we should be very cautious—and we should close the door to change as soon as our test plan is complete. Any change to project results means a different set of tests. There is a danger that we will make errors in changing the test plan. Then we could create something that passes our tests, but still doesn't work for the customer. That is very expensive and we don't want that to happen. So, practice saying, "That's a great idea—and we'll do it as soon as this project is over."

Of course, any one event like this is not a big deal. The problem comes up when we have many alligators, many unforeseen risks, or many bright ideas. How can we prevent this? Good planning, plus education, plus keeping in touch with the project team and the customer.

Creativity is great in planning, but late in the project it is a risk.

127

One thing to watch for is a person or, even more often, a pair—a worker plus a customer—who get excited and keep coming up with new ideas. Even if the ideas are good, they may well not all be doable. Talk to them and explain the trade-off that each new item adds features and value, but only if it works. And if they keep adding features, then there is a very big risk that things won't work. And fancy features that don't work don't add value at all.

Who Asks for More?

A change request can come from anyone on the project. In deciding how to handle the change request, we should consider the source and the motivation for the request. For example:

- ▶ *The senior executive of the customer requests a change.* Listen closely. Ask directly if this is due to a misunderstanding, a change in the customer situation, or a desire for more. Respond accordingly, by either including the change in the project or suggesting that it be done later, in a follow-on project or an upgrade.

- ▶ *The sponsor in the performing company.* Ask for the reason for the change. Maybe your boss wants you to finish up this project quickly, because there's a new client waiting. Find the best way to balance current commitments and corporate priorities.

One Person, out of Control

Sometimes, it's fun to go walking in the woods or out into the city with no plan, just to see what we see and do what we feel like doing. That's a natural human impulse. And that's why even a project done by just one person can get out of control. Think of a time it's happened to you. You start the day with one idea and end up doing something totally different. Are you happy or are you disappointed? That depends on how much your original plans mattered to you.

The point is this: all the sources of scope creep are natural to each of us. If we want to succeed at a project, we need to realize that we can get off track all by ourselves. So, we need to learn to do three things:

- ▶ Remember why we started.
- ▶ Pay attention to what we are doing.
- ▶ Always have a written plan for a project and refer to that plan. Make sure every change happens by choice, not by accident.

The Lesson: Scope creep is natural. Project success takes discipline.

▶ *Someone on the customer team.* Find out if the change is a clarification to the plan, a correction, or a new idea. Unless the change can be included with little change to schedule, cost, and safely, put it off until later.

▶ *Someone on the project team.* Find out if the person is suggesting a new feature that he or she thinks the customer will like. If so, reject the change. But if the customer already wants the change or if the team member is finding a better way of getting work done, include the change if it can be added with little change to the schedule and project cost and at low risk.

▶ *A vendor.* Find out the source of the change. Perhaps an expected supply is no longer available and the change is needed. But if the vendor is pushing something that is better for him or her, such as selling you a new model after you've tested and gotten customer approval for an older one, reject the change as too risky and of no value to the customer.

Managing Scope Creep

Good communications during planning is the best prevention for scope creep.

In project change management, each change requires good judgment. Therefore, it is essential to write down the change request and take it through a process of research, decision, communication, and—if the change is accepted—updating the plan. In addition, we manage the entire load of changes with good communication, planning, and education to prevent scope creep.

Let's close out the chapter with a review of how to prevent scope creep and manage change. Knowing that there are some good reasons for change after the end of the *preparation stage,* we must not close the door to change request. In educating the customer and the team, be clear that, all the way through the project, you want to know what is happening and hear new ideas. It may not be possible to make the requested change, but you always want to consider it. If you don't do that, then some essential change may come up—due to an error in the plan or a change in reality—and no one will tell you because they think you won't make any more changes. So, be sure to keep channels of communication open.

Teach the 1:10:100 rule to everyone you know.

Preventing Scope Creep

In the *preparation stage,* educate everyone about the 1:10:100 rule and set up a clear project life cycle with stages and gates. Let people know that creative ideas are encouraged during the planning and preparation stage. Be sure to do walk-throughs and risk assessment meetings so that features, quality, value, and risks are all addressed in planning. Also, investigate the initial situation as thoroughly as you can. Then make a list of your assumptions and check them. If you do all of this, there will be very few surprises and very few reasons for change.

Seeing Change When It Happens

How do we know when we've changed what we're doing? On a sailing trip, we can't tell where the wind and current are carrying our boat unless we check our location against the stars or against our destination. The same is true on a project. We need to:

▶ Watch what we're doing.

▶ Do a full weekly status-reporting process, even on one-person projects.

▶ Communicate with everyone about what they are finding and what they are doing.

▶ Compare reality with the plan, update status on the plan, and plan and execute any needed corrective action.

When you see a change request or risk event that is more than you can handle within the project scope, schedule, and budget, be sure to manage it well.

Controlling Change Requests

It is reasonable to ask people to write down their change requests, but not reasonable to expect them to do it. We must be ready to listen and then write down the change request ourselves. Any change to scope, no matter how small, should be written down. That way, our project plan and customer and technical documentation remain accurate to what we deliver. If we don't write down every scope change, then our project results are like those irritating consumer appliances for which the instructions don't match. We should do better than that.

If the change affects only scope and we fit it into our current budget and schedule, then we still need to update the quality plan, consider what new tests we need to do, and update the risk plan. And, of course, we need customer approval. If the change requires a change of due date or additional funds, then we need to update our whole project plan and rebaseline the project, as well.

Conclusion: Don't Move the Goalposts

It's easiest to succeed if we stay focused on our original goal. The real keys to success are to plan well and then allow as few changes as possible. I'm not advocating this as a rule for life. I like improvisational music, for example, and on my birthday, my wife and I went walking up a mountain, choosing the route as we went, based on what we saw and what we felt. But, when we're doing a project with a specific goal, we chose that goal because getting there was a better use of our time and money than anything else we could think of. If we remember that, we stay focused and know that, most of the time, changing course in the middle of the trip will cost more, keep us from achieving as much, and lead to disappointment.

Now that we've learned to keep scope under management, let's do the same for time and money in Chapter 15, Stay on Time and on Budget.

Chapter 15

Stay on Time and on Budget

O N A WELL-DEFINED PROJECT, THE STATUS-REPORTING METHOD from Chapter 13, Keeping Everything on Track, is the key to delivering the iron triangle—our complete scope on time and within budget. For the core of the triangle, we track scope against time spent and against money spent. To keep the triangle from being broken, we track quality, risk, communications, and the other issues. In this chapter, we'll take a closer look at tracking and managing time and money in the *doing stage*.

Time Management in the *Doing Stage*

There is a level of technical time management called *critical path analysis* that we don't cover here in *Project Management for Small Business Made Easy*. It helps you figure out which jobs, if delayed, will delay the delivery of the whole project. It matters most when several people are working on a complex project. If you want to learn it, the Project Management Institute will be happy to teach it to you. You can learn more at the web site for this book, www.qualitytechnology.com/DoneRight.

There is one idea from critical path analysis that is important: if you're late on a crucial task, that will push each subsequent step late and you will deliver the project late. Instead of technical analysis, in this chapter we'll focus on practical time management that prevents those delays. We'll do this by looking at two things.

> ► *Managing people and effort.* Remember that effort is the number of person-hours spent doing work.

> ► *Managing deliverables and duration.* Duration is independent of effort. People can be doing a lot of work and it isn't enough. We have to make sure that the project is moving ahead and meeting clear goals from beginning to end.

Managing People and Effort

A friend of mine was asked to teach a class on time management and he answered, "I can't do that, because no one can manage time." When asked to explain what he meant, he asked his customer to look at his watch and tell the second hand to go faster or slower. He pointed out that no one can change what time does, so we can't manage it. But we can change what we do with our time. He'd be happy to teach people how to manage what they do with their time. He got hired for the job.

I would add that we can't manage other people, either. People can only manage themselves. We can bring work under management. We can organize tasks and do all the thinking and planning in the world. But, at the end of planning, project success still boils down to each person doing his or her job on schedule, getting it done well, and delivering it. So we need to guide and support each person toward putting in good effort, toward getting work done on time.

The first step in doing this is to agree on specific tasks from the action plan to be done by a certain date. The worker should agree that the amount of work is reasonable. Check all seven elements of work, as described in Chapter 10, Teamwork and Communications. Also make sure that each person has enough work to do, but not too much.

If you've done that well, then it will be natural for each person to give good status information: "I got these items done. I didn't do this. I did this instead. Here's why." That allows you to compare reality with the plan and

Track work done against time and money spent. Then correct course quickly.

You can't manage time; you can only help people manage what they do with their time.

identify gaps. In Chapter 13, Keeping Everything on Track, we discussed the eight choices you have for adjusting work to the project plan or adjusting the project plan to the way the work is going. For each gap, pick the best solution and give it to your team member.

As you do this, keep these points about effort in mind:

▶ *Any job that isn't defined clearly will be done poorly.* The results won't be what you expected or what the customer needed.

▶ *People will largely do work expected of them.* As a result, all available time will be spent doing assigned tasks. If some tasks were left out of the plan, there won't be time to do them. This is why a complete plan is essential and why you want to encourage team members to think about quality and risk.

In addition to providing specific course correction, we also want to keep our team—and ourselves!—focused and motivated. There are two parts to motivation. One is to remove barriers to motivation. We do this by creating a clear project plan and building the action plan cooperatively with the team. Barriers to motivation arise from lack of clarity or from not having the environment, resources, and other items needed to get a job done.

What if there are no barriers—no de-motivators—but the person still isn't getting the work done? Then we look at the question: How do we help the person be motivated? Here are two things to check:

▶ Does the team member know and remember *why* we are doing the project? The first of our 14 questions, "*Why* are we doing this?" is the key to motivation. Sometimes, our team members and we get lost in the details. Then we need to reconnect with the big picture, the purpose, the *why* of the whole project.

▶ Is it valuable for the team member, as well as for the company? It doesn't work to say, "Do this: it's good for the company" or "Do this: it's good for me or for the team." People will do things to help the company, and you, and the team, but only if it is also good for them, as well. What are you offering? Praise? Appreciation? A small reward, like a dinner out? A promotion or a bonus? Often, praise and appreciation, delivered promptly and clearly, are enough. But there has to be *something* in it for the worker.

If you take care of these, the employee will probably be able to be motivated and focused, put in the effort, and get work done. If you still run into problems, then here are some larger issues to watch out for:

▶ *Interruptions or conflicting priorities.* When people get interrupted, they work only one-third as fast as if they are not interrupted. Also, they may be given contradictory priorities between the project and other work or may feel that there is a conflict. Work to clear time and clarify priorities.

▶ *The need for a can-do attitude.* A can-do attitude, also called a proactive approach, is essential for project work. Because projects are unique, they bring up new challenges and demand creative thinking. Support this in your team. If any team members are more "I just do my job," focus on having them understand that there is no excuse for missing a deadline. If work gets stuck, then there is a reason, and team members should come to you and bring the problems, so you can get the work unstuck and they can meet their goals.

▶ *Overestimation of speed or ability.* The plan may simply have had an over-optimistic estimate. Rather than continuing to accept a small, cumulative delay each week, ask what you've learned about how much work can be done and revise the plan so that it is realistic.

If these issues are resolved, project work will almost certainly go well. If it doesn't, then some larger issue—personal or at work—is getting in the way. It isn't a project problem; it's a general management problem getting in the way of the problem. Check out my book, *Perfect Solutions for Difficult Employee Situations,* for an effective approach to these issues.

Managing Deliverables and Duration

Very few people really understand what happens when one deliverable—one piece of work—is a bit late or isn't quite right and requires rework. Mostly, we think, "Oh, I'm an hour—or half a day—behind. I'll catch up." But, on a project, it doesn't work that way. Tasks are interconnected: Task #2 can't start until the input from Task #1 is complete and correct.

It's like catching a series of trains on a schedule. We may miss the first train by only an hour, but then we have to wait a day for the next scheduled train on that route. And we arrive a day late at the first city. But that means

Keep the train on the track. Once it's off, a long time will go by before it's moving again.

135

we miss the weekly market, so we stay an extra week. Then it turns out we hit a local holiday, so we can't go from our first city to the second city for yet another week. So a one-hour delay puts us two weeks behind.

Project tasks and tests and review meetings are coordinated like train schedules; once we're running late, we'll keep getting further and further behind.

And rushing isn't a solution. When we rush, we do shoddy work. That requires rework, which puts us even further behind. Project success requires that a project team run like a well-oiled machine. As project managers, we grease the gears by eliminating all hassle.

Here are some basic points about work and deliverables to share with your team.

▶ *Prepare, do, follow through* works for every task, no matter how small. Visualize your work and check your inputs before you start.

▶ *Prepare ahead of time if you can.* A great way to finish your workday is to check and make sure that your plan and your inputs are clear for the next day of work.

Where's the Box?

One of the most complicated projects I've ever worked on involved upgrading 70 computer networks all around the country at the same time. At each location, when the vendor had prepared the phone line, we would send all the computer equipment. When that arrived, we would send an installer with a mission: get in, get the network running, and get out so you can fly to the next job. Before the installer flew out, we would always call the remote office to make sure that they got all the equipment. One time, we had done this, but there was a change of schedule and the installer arrived two weeks later. He checked the equipment and found that one item—a router, which is the first thing he had to install to make everything else work—wasn't there. He looked everywhere. He called us and we confirmed it had been there two weeks ago.

To make a long story short, he spent half a day looking for that box. Finally, he found it under the secretary's desk, propping up a small electric heater. She thought it was just the right size to use to keep her feet warm!

I'm not sure the worker could stay late to get the job done at that particular facility. If not, losing the half-day hunting for the box meant spending an extra day at that location, which meant rearranging the installer's travel schedule for the next two weeks.

The Lesson: Time is lost in the details. A missed item is a missed deadline. A missed deadline cascades into a delayed project.

▶ *No task is done until it is tested and then reworked and retested if necessary.* Skipping tests and shoddy work are not options. If you can't get it tested and done right, let the project manager know that you're running behind.

▶ *Work to prevent delays, but don't hide delays.* If you're going to be late—if you even might be late—say so. The sooner you let the project manager know, the better.

▶ *Commit to completion.* Own your work, focus on success, and do what it takes. You'll do as well as you believe you can.

When we offer these basic points to our teams, we have to hold up our end. We have to be consistently willing to hear bad news, appreciate being told, and then calmly take care of things in a reasonable way. We should do our best to work with people respectfully, even when we are frustrated and our goals are not met. If we do that, we can explain the real consequences to our workers. I've found that when I do that, workers respond with loyalty and continuously improving effort.

That attitude of goal-oriented teamwork produces *Team Success*™. With a strong project team, we can handle the unexpected events and delays that are sure to come up just because people are people and because life is what it is.

Cost Management in the *Doing Stage*

The biggest challenge in project cost management for small business is getting billed, paying our bills, and keeping things totted up as we go along. Traditional accounting doesn't mind running months behind, as long as the numbers come out right in the end. Some small businesses don't worry about bookkeeping until the end of the month, or even not until taxes are due. But, in project management, we need to make decisions based on up-to-date information every week.

Don't wait for the book-keeper. Track your money as you spend it.

In small business project management, you have three choices for tracking project expenses:

▶ *Set up a small budget and expense spreadsheet for the project* and track purchasing and expenses there. Update your information as you spend the money or weekly.

▶ *Use a small business accounting system.* If you don't already use account codes, add them to the system. Your accountant or an experienced bookkeeper can show you how to set up account codes. Then enter transactions as you spend the money or weekly.

▶ *Don't track expenses as you go—and be ready for some nasty surprises.* If you don't keep on top of expenses, then, at some point, maybe after the project is over, the bills will pile up. You'll probably discover you were way over budget because you didn't keep costs under management.

Simply tracking expenses is an important first step. There are four other things you can do to keep costs under management and also reduce hassle.

▶ *Do clear procurement in writing.* Even for small items and short, inexpensive sub-contractor jobs, write a letter of agreement saying what will be done, when it will be done, and how much it will cost. Send it out right after the phone call or meeting that set up the work, by e-mail or regular mail. Make sure that the purchasing paperwork and the budget match one another. For example, if there was a price negotiation as you chose your vendor, adjust the budget in your spreadsheet or accounting system to match the price you agreed on.

▶ *Keep up to date with vendors.* Agree on schedules for billing and work with vendors. In some industries, a deposit before work begins is customary. In others, you pay for deliverables. In that case, be sure to be clear that you will pay for deliverables after review and acceptance, not on delivery. You want to make sure the work is good before you pay. Ask for prompt billing; if you don't get it, exchange e-mails or letters stating the current account balance, so that your weekly expense status is verified against what the vendors are expecting.

▶ *Keep organized electronic and paper files.* I'll admit I'm not always good on this one. I keep all electronic files and in pretty good order. But when I slip on the paper files, I pay the price in hassle and lost time. When a vendor forgets a request or a signed contract gets lost in the mail, if I have good files, I can send a replacement right away and keep things moving. But if my office is a mess, I have to interrupt myself and endure a lot of hassle and inefficiency to keep things going.

But I Didn't Spend a Million Dollars!

This is a true story from a project manager at an insurance company. The company had an excellent computerized accounting system, but it was designed for managing insurance claims, not managing projects. The accounting department really only cared if the annual books were correct. A project manager was running a project with a budget of about $1.4 million. He bought new computer for $1 million. Someone made a data-entry error and charged the $1 million expense twice. As a result, it looked like the project manager was way over budget, when he was right on target to spend the rest of the money and finish the project.

Unfortunately, due to the accounting error, all his actual expense records were off by $1 million, and his projections and forecasts couldn't be done easily. He asked the accounting department to correct the error and they said that they could do that only after the accounting year was closed, several months after the project was due. The accounting department could not understand that the long delay was a problem. It was the way they always did business.

Meanwhile, week by week, the project manager got further and further behind because, every time he tried to make a small purchase, he had to explain that there really was still money in his budget. He and his bosses looked bad because they looked like they'd blown their budget, too.

It's stories like this that make me glad I work for a small company!

The Lesson: Traditional accounting methods and normal small-business book-keeping are not good enough for projects. We need to track spending in real time, week by week.

▶ *Price shop and negotiate for discounts.* Up until now, I've urged for a focus on quality and reliability in vendors and products, even if that means paying a premium price. I do that because, in my own experience, we end up paying more for the project and running into lots of hassles and delays if we rely on lower-quality products and unreliable vendors. However, if we can ensure sufficient quality and reliability, it makes sense to get the best price we can, as long as we think it is worth our time. Here are some techniques:

  – *Price shopping.* If we define a particular item we want to buy, down to the exact model with specific features, we can look for the least expensive reliable vendor. That's very easy to do on the internet these days. If a vendor helped you choose the product, it is a courtesy to go back to that vendor and say, "I appreciate your help in choosing this product. I'd like to buy from you, but the best price I could find is lower. If you can match that price, I'll buy from you."

– *Negotiation*. If we have multiple acceptable vendors, we can negotiate among them for a better price. If we have only one vendor, we may be able to arrange a deal, especially if we are looking at more work in the future or if we can offer them some kind of support, such as referrals and references, in return for a job well done.

Conclusion: The Iron Triangle Delivered

All the work, on time, and within budget.

Each project is different. On some, cost is a major issue; on others, it hardly matters. We should decide how important tracking time and cost on a project is to the company and then work accordingly. Using these techniques, we track time and expenses as we go, increase the chances of completing on time, reduce cost, and reduce hassle. We must track work completed against time, at least, to some degree. Otherwise, work will not remain under management and the project will get left aside as other, apparently more urgent things come up. If we track work done against time and money each week, we can make sure that the project is getting done on time and under budget.

As we will see in the next three chapters, it is also important to manage quality so that we eliminate error and increase value, manage risk to make sure that the project gets done, and manage expectations, so that the customer is happy, getting what he or she asked for. If we do all of these things, we keep the project well under control in the *doing stage* and we're right in line for successful completion.

Chapter 16

Quality: Eliminate Error

I N CHAPTER 8, MAKING IT GOOD, WE TALKED ABOUT QUALITY PLANNING and emphasized that focusing on quality from the beginning actually lowers project cost while improving the quality of results and allows us to finish the project sooner by eliminating time-wasting hassle. Now, we'll carry that forward into the *doing stage* by learning these methods:

▶ *Creating work systems that eliminate error.* All work systems either allow more error or keep it out and allow you to eliminate more and more error as you go. Most companies waste time with methods that were outmoded a century ago. In this section, you'll learn how to create effective, efficient work systems.

▶ *Creating a quality team.* Quality can be achieved only if each person works for it and if we work toward it as a team as well. We'll show you how to create a highly effective, quality team.

▶ *Ensuring quality at all three levels of work.* On a project, we have to pay attention to ensuring business and customer value, achieving project goals, and doing good technical work. We'll show you how quality management is applied at all three levels.

Quality pays off and it's fund, too!

The field of quality management gives us many tools to be effective—to do the right job and add value—and to be efficient—to do the job right, reducing time spent and money spent. A focus on quality also gives us pride in our work and eliminates hassle, so we feel professional and enjoy getting good work done.

Work Systems That Eliminate Error

The way we work either reduces error or lets error pile up.

In setting up the way we do work, whether for projects or for routine work, we should design the flow of the work so that every job is done once and information and parts move automatically from one step to the next without any need for rework. As we work more and more with information and computers, this becomes easier.

I'll use writing and publishing as my example, because, these days, almost every company uses the written word. We deliver fliers, web sites, customer guides, and all kinds of other written products to our customers. And everything I say here applies to audio recordings, video, and movies as well.

Back before personal computers, a writer had to type a manuscript and then retype it for any major changes. Then an editor had to mark it up and a typesetter had to retype every word into a special machine that would compose the book. If you go back even further, each letter had to be set as a piece of type into a page for a printing press. In those days, rework was unavoidable. And, with every step of rework, it was possible that new errors would be added. So, an author would write a draft with some mistakes. He would edit out the mistakes and then retype, putting in new mistakes. The editor would

100 Years Behind the Times

When I was researching my book, *Quality Management Demystified,* I discovered that a fellow named Frederick Winslow Taylor figured out how to get work done right and published his treatise on *Scientific Management* in 1911. In quality management, we've spent about 100 years learning to put his ideas into practice. The keys are to define quality, have work practices in writing, measure results, and keep improving our process to improve our results. It works because the way we work, very simply, determines what we get.

The Lesson: Many companies, large and small, are still using techniques from the 1800s. Learn quality management to apply the best of the scientific method and make huge improvements in results and profit.

edit out those mistakes, and then the compositor would add new ones. This process would go on and on, eliminating mistakes and then adding more.

The process of checking something to eliminate errors is called *inspection*. Inspection can be automated—done by machine—or it can be done by people. Human inspection, even in the best of circumstances, misses lots of errors. As a result, the key to creating a process that eliminates errors is to eliminate rework by automating communication of information and transfer of parts and then to automate as much inspection as possible.

How is this done in publishing in the best work environments today? The author types onto a computer and makes changes without retyping. Then the editor makes changes without retyping. Computerized compositors—also known as desktop publishing programs—lay out the pages, formatting text and graphics and making a manuscript ready for printing in computer files that go straight to a printing press.

Using this method takes more than buying computers and software. We also have to change the way we work, the process. If editors—and I know some who are like this—still print out copy and mark it up, then redraw graphics instead of handling graphics files, they don't take advantage of many of the benefits of using better tools because they're working with old processes that require rework and let error into the process.

When it comes to inspection, the best solution for most small business projects is to combine human inspection with automated inspection. In publishing, this means that we still need an editor and a proofreader, but we use spellcheckers and automatic search-and-replace to make the text correct and consistent and we let the humans focus on the tasks that only humans can do.

The problem is that many companies pay some attention to tools, but few pay enough attention to process. In project management, we can improve our work processes by looking at our action plan. Here are the questions we should ask:

▶ Is any job being done more than once?

▶ Is every deliverable being checked as thoroughly as possible for correctness before it is used in next step?

▶ Are all problems written down in one place so we can keep track of them?

▶ Do we make sure to resolve every problem?

143

▶ Do we look at our list of problems to find and prevent repeating problems?

If we are not doing all of these things, we should change our work processes so that we are. Improving process this way typically eliminates 20 percent to 40 percent of the effort spent on a project. Imagine every project being done in only 60 percent to 80 percent of the time it now takes. Imagine saving 20 percent to 40 percent on every project budget. Even more important, imagine finding your work hassle-free, so that you can focus on making things better, instead of on just getting the job done. These are the benefits of applying quality management to our projects.

Plan, Do, Check, Act (PDCA)

One of the most basic ideas behind science is *empiricism,* the idea that we can learn by observing and experimenting. In science, the goals are to learn why things are the way they are and how things work. Empiricism is applied through the *scientific method,* where we observe reality, create a *hypothesis*— a potential reason for things being the way they are—and then design and develop an *experiment* to test the hypothesis. When a hypothesis is well tested and found to be the best explanation, we call it a *theory.* When a broad, general theory stands the test of time, we call it a *scientific law.* But even laws are subject to change. Newton's law of gravity was challenged by empirical evidence and replaced by a more accurate theory, Einstein's theory of relativity.

In business, we're concerned with making things work well, not with how things work. But we can apply the scientific method to business and engineering questions quite well. The scientific method was applied to engineering in the mid-1700s by John Smeaton. It was applied to work processes by Taylor in the late 1800s. And it was simplified into a business system that any worker could use by Walter A. Shewhart in the 1920s. That simple system is PDCA.

PDCA was popularized by W. Edwards Deming, the founder of the Total Quality Management (TQM) movement, improved in Japan from 1950 to 1980 as part of the Japanese continuous improvement movement, and brought back to the U.S. by Deming in 1980.

I think that every small business benefits when all of its employees learn and use PDCA. It works like this:

▶ *Plan.* Look at a piece of work to be done or a business problem and decide what you are going to do. Sometimes, the course of action is obvious and clear. Other times, it involves research into the problem or learning methods for solving the problem.

▶ *Do*. We perform the plan, doing the work we think will get the job done or solve the problem.

▶ *Check*. We evaluate. Did we really get the job done? Did we really solve the problem? Are we satisfied with the results of our planning and doing?

▶ *Act*. We take action based on the checking, as follows:
  – If we like the results—if checking gave us a thumbs-up—we make our plan the standard plan for doing this work or solving this problem.
  – If we don't like the results—if checking gave us a thumbs-down—then we revise the plan and try again. That is, we repeat the PDCA cycle until we understand the problem and have a good way to solve it or until we have the most effective and efficient way to get work done.

PDCA is simple and it works on any size of problem. It works in planning how to run a company, it works in planning a project or a stage of a project, and it works all the way down to a simple task on our action plan that might take two hours or a little problem that pops up and gets in the way of our work. After we talk about how to create a quality team for your project or business, we'll see how PDCA can be used to ensure success on the business level, the project management level, and the technical level of each project.

Creating a Quality Team

In Chapter 10, Teamwork and Communications, we talked about the *Success Team™* approach to goal-oriented teamwork. We can take this one step further by adding an individual and team focus on quality and value. Indeed, we can achieve quality only if each individual and the team are focused on creating quality and delivering value. Here's how this works:

Quality is achieved only by combining individual and team effort.

▶ Each person wants to do good work, focuses on doing good work, and does these things:
  – Plans carefully, taking responsibility for ensuring that he or she has all the elements necessary for successful work.
  – Ensures the value of his or her deliverables by getting the specifications

145

defined by the people who will use those outputs as inputs for their processes.

- Checks work results before delivery to ensure they meet the specifications and delivers the right result on time, using PDCA.
- Uses PDCA to improve his or her own work processes.

▶ The team members together do these things:

- Plan work by defining the quality of each deliverable as what is needed for its use as input of the next process.
- Check each other's work and offer their work to be checked by each other.
- Check their inputs as soon as they are available, so that rework, when it is needed, is done right away.

▶ The project manager does these things:

- Defines value for the whole project and lets the team know the benefits the customers and the company will receive as a result of the project.
- Defines a work flow for the project that is free of hassles and eliminates errors.
- Keeps hassles out of the way, ensuring that each team member has all that is needed to do the job and focus on quality.
- Appreciates and rewards quality work.
- Listens to the team members and uses ideas from the team for quality improvements.

There are always errors. The only question is "Do you want your team members to find them so you can fix them, or do you want the customer to find them?"

As project managers, we create and maintain a team focus on quality by:

▶ Leading by example.

▶ Teaching fundamentals of quality.

▶ Setting up fair team rules that create quality results. For example, don't just check the work that certain people do. Instead, make a rule that says, "Everything will be checked by two people before it leaves the company."

▶ Accepting error without criticizing people, yet also be honest and clear about the cost of error and continuously learn and teach new ways to prevent and eliminate error.

There is no end to the amount of improvement we can make by focusing on quality. We can do this in two ways. Some companies focus on *continuous improvement,* which has everyone on the team constantly doing their best work and constantly using PDCA to do even better work. Other companies focus on *quality breakthroughs,* using experts to bring in new technology and methods to radically improve effectiveness and efficiency. Both methods work very well.

Small businesses can do both. What's the best place to start? Use the methods in this chapter to build a quality team and you put your company on the path to continuous improvement.

So, we've set up a work flow that eliminates hassle and rework and focuses on preventing and eliminating error. We've learned PDCA and taught it to our team, so our quality team is ready to go. Now, we'll see how to apply quality to the whole project, top to bottom, to the business level, the project level, and the technical level.

Quality at the Business Level

We focus on the business level of quality more in planning the project and in follow-through at the end than we do during the *doing stage* in the middle. Quality planning at the business level means defining project results that, when delivered, will offer the greatest possible value. As a result, we ensure that business value in the *doing stage* by delivering to specification on time and within budget, that is, by focusing on quality at the project and technical levels.

Add value for the customer and for your own company.

There are some things to monitor for quality at the business level during the *doing stage.* If any of these become issues, we should respond promptly and effectively to ensure the business value of the project:

▶ *A change to the customer or the company may require a change in project goals, timeline, or budget.* Responsiveness is part of quality. If the product we are creating won't work for the customer or the company as a result of a change to the customer or the company, then we should adjust the product specification so that the customer will realize value from the result. If the customer will suddenly benefit from early delivery, we should consider that and do it if it is feasible— charging an extra fee, if appropriate. If the customer or the company suddenly hits hard time and can't get money for the project, we should advocate for the project and also create a solution that works for the customer.

▶ *Clarify or resolve any misunderstanding in the definition of the prod-*

uct or service. Define the issue and then ask, "What reasonable, workable solution adds greatest value to the customer and the company?"

▶ *Focus on value.* Every worker, in making the small decisions that come up in interpreting any specification, should ask, "What will work best for the customer?" If it's affordable, we talk to the customers and get their answer to those questions as we start each piece of work or discover each issue.

The PDCA Business Model

PDCA is a simple model for an entire business:

▶ *Plan.* Design a product or service for sale.
▶ *Do.* Create the product or service, market it, and sell it.
▶ *Check.* See how well it sells. See if it meets customer requirements. See if customers like it and how you can make it better for them.
▶ *Act.* Make those improvements and do a better job selling a better product or service.

In fact, PDCA was first defined as a business cycle. Later, quality and process managers realized that it could apply to projects and technical work as well.

Quality at the Project Level

Here's a good question: How do we know we are doing all we reasonably can to make sure we are doing a good job? The answer is a method called *quality assurance.* Quality assurance (QA) focuses on planning and process: there are many techniques for making sure that we are working in the most effective and efficient ways.

Good project process leads to project success.

QA tools are most valuable for ensuring quality at the project level. Here are some valuable tools and techniques:

▶ *Forms and templates.* Use forms and templates like the ones at the back of this book as reminders of the questions to ask and the things to think about in project planning, status reporting, and other project management work. You can get these forms in electronic version, and lots more, at www.qualitytechnology.com/DoneRight.

▶ *Checklists.* Turn action plans into checklists so people can actually check off work as it is done. Have checklists for routine project planning and management tasks, such as a checklist for making sure you are prepared to do a job and another one to make sure you've finished a job.

▶ *Reviews.* During our gate reviews, we should look at the project process, not only at results. Are status meetings effective? Is communication good? Are any problems not being discussed? We can also do a more in-depth review if the project isn't going well.

In addition to QA, we apply PDCA at the project level through the weekly status-reporting and corrective-action process described in Chapter 13, Keeping Everything on Track. With these tools, we can assure ourselves that we are managing all nine areas of project management for the project all the way through the *doing stage*.

Quality at the Technical Level

Have you ever had a friendly, efficient company receive your order, then deliver a product right on time—but it's not what you ordered, it's something else entirely? Not much good, is it? That's what will happen on your project if you do good quality work at the business and project levels, but not at the technical level. All of our focus on value and process supports delivering the right thing, in working order, on time.

If you're going to make something, make it work.

To make sure that we make the right thing and that it works, we focus on quality at the technical level and we use tools from *quality control*. Quality control (QC) is the process of inspecting, checking, and testing work results and using the results of those inspections, checks, and tests to do two things:

▶ *Take corrective action.* We fix what isn't working or we scrap it and do it again.

▶ *Inform the QA process so action can be taken to prevent similar errors and defects.* QC checking, inspection, and testing is of little value if we just use it to fix this one item. It is really valuable when we also use it to learn a lesson, then take action to prevent similar problems in the future.

QC work applies to more than just what we deliver to the customer. It also applies to technical specifications and even to the project planning documents.

So QC is mostly for the technical level of the project, but it also applies to the project management level. And, on large projects, we may find that there is some repetitive work, so we can apply QA at the technical level as well.

A whole book could be written about how to prepare technical test plans, but we have room for just a quick note here. Here are some good things to do when making a test plan:

▶ Make the test plan before you start building the product.

▶ Make the test plan to test every benefit, feature, and function defined in your scope statement and WBS.

▶ Test the product, its instructions, and its technical documentation.

▶ Test to make sure the product is easy for the customer to understand, install, use, and support.

▶ Test to make sure the product is reliable, is easy to fix, and survives damage and disaster.

▶ Test marketing materials as well, if you are promoting or selling project results.

▶ Whenever affordable, include customers in the testing.

PDCA in quality management at the technical level is a day-by-day approach to each task, and can also be used by a team member or the whole team to address problems that come up during the project.

Conclusion: Quality All the Way Through

Quality top to bottom, quality beginning to end.

If we plan for quality as we discussed in Chapter 8, Making It Good, and then we work to prevent and eliminate error and produce quality in the *doing stage* as we learned in this chapter, and then we deliver quality in the *follow-through* stage as you will learn about in Chapters 19 and 20, we've done quality from top to bottom and quality from beginning to end. Companies that work this way delight their customers and show astounding business results. I hope yours will be one of them.

Now, we turn our focus to making sure things go right in Chapter 17, Risk: Manage Uncertainty.

Chapter 17

Risk: Manage Uncertainty

WHEN YOU COMPLETED THE RISK LIST DESCRIBED IN CHAPTER 9, Making Sure the Job Gets Done, you prepared for the risk management work of the *doing stage* of the project. Now, we'll learn how to manage risk actively and proactively using these steps:

▶ *Watch for risks* every week, at the status meeting, and every day as well.

▶ *Monitor risk status* and track it accurately.

▶ *Keep looking ahead* for new risks.

▶ *Manage risks quickly* when triggers occur.

▶ *Keep the project moving* when the stuff hits the fan and you have to manage risk events as well.

Watch for Risks

Most project managers don't even take the time to create a list of risks, so, if you and your team have done the planning recommended in Chapter 9, Making Sure the Job Gets Done, you are already ahead of the game. But staying ahead of the game requires keeping an eye out for risks throughout the project. Having a risk and not managing risks every week and every day is like owning a fire extinguisher and keeping it buried at the bottom of your closet.

Anyone who's ever read an adventure story or watched a Western or a World War II movie knows that, when your squad is in the field, you have to keep a lookout at night. You also have a point man or woman watching for trouble and a rear guard watching your back while you're on the move. Well, in the *doing stage* of a project, we're in the field and on the move. So let's work as a team, watch our backs, and keep a lookout ahead.

This seems pretty basic. So it makes sense to ask, if it is basic, why do so few people do it? Why do project managers get blindsided by sudden events, even ones that they thought would happen? If we understand why, maybe we can help our team change its habits. Here are some reasons:

▶ *We're used to hassle, so we just live with it.* In most work environments, things almost always go wrong and, when we try to fix them, something goes wrong with the fix. Since we'll never solve the problem, we don't even try. That's unfortunate but livable in routine work—at least until the costs make you uncompetitive and you go out of business. But, on a project, there's a deadline and the little hassles add up more quickly, so failure comes sooner.

▶ *We always think we can catch up.* Each problem is usually so little that we're like the fabled frog in the pan of water on the stove. The frog got warmed so slowly that he didn't sense the danger and jump to safety, so he boiled to death. We get behind a little bit at a time. By the time we acknowledge it, it's too late to save the project.

▶ *There are just too many interruptions.* If we're managing multiple projects, or if we handle customer service, or we just don't have all of our work organized, we get hit with one thing after another after another. We're lost in work overload or information overload.

Every team member should keep an eye out for risks.

Unfortunately, all of these problems are all too familiar for most of us. What's the solution? I would suggest the following:

▶ *A realistic, optimistic attitude.* Yes, problems are real. Yes, people can solve problems.

▶ *A team approach.* Organize the team so that one or two people handle interruptions at certain times, so others can get work done. (You can rotate mornings and afternoons or day by day.) Realize that each of us will get slammed at one time or another, so it makes sense for all of us to pitch in and help each other out.

▶ *A reality check*. We should measure our real progress accurately against our plan, so we know exactly how much the little things are piling up.

▶ *PDCA*. Identify a problem, then solve it. Do that again. And again. The number of problems is huge sometimes, but it's never infinite.

Monitor Risk Status

Our list of risks is a tool, just like the kitchen sponge. Once a day—or more often—we take out the kitchen sponge and wipe the counter. Just the same, once a week—or more often—at the status meeting, we should take out our risk list and actively monitor each risk on the list and any new ones as well.

Every week, check your risk list against reality.

At any given time during the project, each risk has a status. Here are the possible statuses:

▶ It hasn't happened yet but it still could.

▶ It could happen any time now.

▶ Here it is! The risk trigger has happened.

▶ The risk event is happening and it's out of control.

▶ The risk event is happening and it's under management.

▶ The risk event happened and we took care of it.

▶ The risk event never happened and we're past the danger point; it can't happen now.

Every week, we should have a note on our risk plan next to each risk, identifying the status of that risk.

Keep Looking Ahead

Managing the risks on our list isn't enough. One way to understand risk management is to say that the future is always unknown. As we walk into it, if we have a risk list, those risks are our *known unknowns*. But there are other things that could happen, things we didn't expect at all. Those are the *unknown unknowns*.

Ships sailing through fog keep a lookout.

We and our team need to keep an eye out for anything that could change the way we have to do the project, whether it's on the list or not. We even need to keep an eye out for unexpected good news. Good news for a project can still require action, which means we have to change our project schedule to take advantage of the good news and realize the opportunity it offers.

Good News Can Really Ruin Your Day

Just recently, I was working on a very tight deadline for one part of a project. In the middle of the day of the deadline, I got an e-mail that told me of a wonderful opportunity to really boost sales on the same project, but only if I jumped out and did several hours of work immediately. The opportunity was unexpected, in spite of my best efforts. (I'd been told the opportunity was several weeks away.) So I jumped and I called up two members of my team to jump with me. We got the work done and realized the opportunity—and then I dove into a late night of work to meet the job deadline.

The Lesson: Don't let success or troubles get in your way. Get the team members together and do what it takes to *get it done right!*

Manage Risks Quickly

The sooner we act, the less time and money we lose.

So the stuff hits the fan. The trigger is triggered. Now what? The answer is … PDCA, fast.

Think of notification of a risk trigger as an alarm bell going off at a fire station. Until we respond, the fire is out of control. Of course, most risks are neither as dangerous nor as fast-acting as a fire, but our attitude and approach should be the same. Here are the steps we take:

▶ *Identify the risk,* both in reality and on the risk plan.

▶ *Find out exactly what is going on.*

▶ *Check the plan.* We may already have a contingency plan, thought out in calmer times, that tells us what to do.

▶ *Plan.* Decide clearly what to do. The plan can be flexible, but it must be clear. For example, it isn't enough to say, "Call so-and-so and find out what happened." Instead, our plan is "Call so-and-so and find out if A happened or if B happened. If A happened, tell so-and-so to do this. If B happened, meet so-and-so tomorrow morning and do that together. If something else altogether happened, figure out what is going on."

154

- *Do.* Take the action meant to bring the situation under control.

- *Check.* Is the situation under control? Do you know what is going on and what to do next? If not, keep working to bring the situation under control. If so, take a breath and ask, "What should I focus on now—the risk event or the project?"

- *Act.* Update the risk plan; then continue with appropriate corrective action.

- *PDCA again.* Focusing on either the risk event or the project, plan what do to next—and go from there.

Way Too Many Things Going Wrong

I just got a phone call from a friend who had to leave his business for several months. He left it in the hands of a capable worker who he thought could manage things in his absence. He's just gotten back into the country. He checked things out, but hasn't made it into his office yet. All he knows right now is that operating expenses are several thousand dollars higher than they should be—twice as high as expected, in fact. That looks like a big problem.

It isn't. It's a lot of little problems. It may be half a dozen problems or it may be two dozen. Very soon, he'll be back at the office and he'll be able to find out what each problem is. One at a time, he'll pay each bill or dispute it. One at a time, he'll find out why each bill was so high and figure out what he needs to do to make sure it doesn't happen again. While he's doing that, his worker will work hard and stir up more jobs, helping bring in some extra cash to make the business work again. If he keeps working through each detail using PDCA, he'll probably be in very good shape when busy season comes around in a few months.

How do I know? Because I had to do the same thing three years ago when my mother got sick and I had to set my business aside to go take care of her. These kinds of things are the blessing and challenge of the independence of owning a small business. I could take the time off to do what mattered most. Then I had to start all over and make things work. If you have to, I'm sure you can do it, too.

The Lesson: When things get very challenging, break the work up into very small pieces. Then solve each one with PDCA.

Keep the Project Moving

The point of risk management is not to manage risks; it is to succeed in delivering project results on time and within budget, or reasonably close to that, in spite of risk events. So, when a risk event happens, we have to take care of both the risk event and the project.

For small risk events, that's pretty simple. We take some hours aside to deal with the risk event, and then we get back to the project. For moderate-sized risks for which it is clear what action to take, we do a similar thing, except that we should need to plan who should work on the risk event and who should do project work, and also which tasks we can afford to delay while the risk event is being managed.

Larger risk events take more careful management. Risk events that are harder to bring under control need more careful management, too. In these cases, the best approach is to divide and conquer: one person handles the risk event while another handles the project. Here's how to decide who should do which job:

▶ *If the problem is technical,* then let a technical team member handle the risk event while you keep the project rolling.

▶ *If the problem is with a customer or is related to management,* then you should manage the risk event and turn day-to-day project management and status meetings over to a team leader.

To prepare for the second possibility, it is good to train team members in status reporting and routine project management skills. A capable self-manager with a bit of team management experience can probably handle a project in the *doing stage* for a short period, as long as you provide support and guidance. Once the risk event is under control, you can take back management of the project.

If you are running a one-person project, a major risk event happens, and you can't clone yourself, what do you do?

▶ *Bring the risk event under control* by finding out what is happening and doing what must be done right away.

▶ *Update your plan,* so that you know exactly where you are.

▶ *Come up with some options.*

- ▶ *Inform everyone involved* in the project and in any other deadlines you have. Explain that something big is up. Find out who has leeway and who doesn't. You may find that some people are unexpectedly generous or that someone else is running behind on his or her part of the work, so that a delay on your side doesn't matter.

- ▶ *Decide what option costs the least to your business.*

- ▶ *Implement that option,* whether it's to delay the project, cancel the project, put the project on hold, or spend a bunch of sleepless nights.

- ▶ *Inform everyone* that you're working in what I call "crisis mode."

- ▶ *Focus on getting each job done,* one at a time.

But What About a Disaster?

A risk event is not a disaster. A risk event is something that has at least a fair chance of happening during a project that will force a change in the project. A disaster is a big, rare event that is unlikely. Disaster preparedness, often called *business continuity planning,* is a whole different topic. And, when a disaster happens, it requires a whole different approach than the reaction to a risk event being triggered.

In case of a business disaster, decide what is best for the business. It might be best to cancel the project or put it on hold. Or, it might be best to continue. Face the disaster, continue your business, and make choices that make things safe through the storm and increase your chances of clearing away the damage and rebuilding afterwards.

Of course, risk events take effort, the work to handle the risks costs money, sometimes there are other expenses, and sometimes they cause us to miss deadlines and delay project delivery. We should take our risk plan into account when creating the project schedule and budget. It is unrealistic to expect no risk events to occur, just as it is unrealistic to think that they will all happen. Technically, this extra time and money to handle risk events is called a *contingency* in our schedule and budget. Practically, as long as we are within those contingencies, our project is on time and within budget. If the risk events are so large or so numerous that we can't get the whole job done on time and within budget, then we will know it as soon as we can, because we are tracking all of this as we go. And, when we know it, we can escalate from project risk management to project change management. We revise our plan, either adding time and money to make it all the way to the end of the project or dropping something from the scope, as we discussed in Chapter 13, Keeping Everything on Track.

Conclusion: Sailing Through Stormy Waters

If you don't sink and you keep moving in the right direction, eventually you'll get to your destination.

Just like sailing trips, some projects are easier than others. If you have a fair wind and clear weather, wonderful! But that isn't a reason not to pack life preservers and storm sails, not to practice using them, or not to keep a storm watch. Risk readiness pays off as soon as a storm hits. Preparedness, fast response, and a strong hand at the helm to steady the ship through the storm while moving in the right direction as best we can will allow us to reach our destination. That's the beauty of PDCA: as long as we're moving more or less in the right direction, even slowly, we can keep correcting course and speed until all the work is done and we deliver the scope of the project on time and on budget or with planned, approved changes that we may need to make.

We've now learned all that there is to know to manage our project through the *doing stage*. However, we also have to manage our customers in the *doing stage*—and that is the subject of Chapter 18, Managing Expectations.

Chapter 18

Managing Expectations

I**T IS PERFECTLY POSSIBLE TO DEFINE A PROJECT CORRECTLY, DO THE RIGHT** job, and deliver to specification on time and within budget—and for the project to be a total disaster. Why? Because it is not enough to meet the customers' specifications; we have to meet their expectations as well.

Expectations are often unspoken. Like unwritten assumptions, unspoken expectations can be the death of a project. If we want to satisfy our customers by delivering project results, we need to bring expectations under management. We can do this if we take the following steps:

- ▶ Discuss expectations openly.
- ▶ Document expectations into the specification.
- ▶ Define the expectations gap.
- ▶ Manage the expectations gap with gate reviews that include the customers.
- ▶ Ensure ongoing communication with all customers.

If we take these five steps, we will manage expectations and prepare for achieving customer delight, the topic of Chapter 20.

Discuss Expectations Openly

I am perpetually amazed by how much well-meaning professionals who think clearly misunderstand one another. Some of the problems come from not taking the time to explore and listen well enough. Some of the problems come because we have different professional backgrounds and areas of expertise, so that our assumptions are different. As a result, what one person calls "expensive" another calls "cheap." For example, when I was moving to San Antonio, a real estate agent was afraid to show me the type of rental property I wanted. She thought I would turn white when I heard the price. But I'd lived in Manhattan and paid about the same rent for less than half the space. She not only didn't try to find out what my assumptions were, but actively avoided getting them. I had to insist that, in the San Antonio market, price was not an issue. Only then did I get what I wanted.

We can do better than that. We need to open honest dialog about expectations and assumptions. When we do, we need to explain that there will be misunderstandings and that we want to find them early and prevent them from creeping in. We will do this in three steps:

▶ In the *preparation stage,* we define terms clearly and define precisely what the customer wants, turning expectations into specifications.

▶ In the *doing stage,* we maintain communications, so that expectations remain clear and are coordinated with the specification and so that any necessary changes get into the project plan.

▶ In the *follow-through stage,* we bring the product, service, or project result and the customer together and we take time to ensure that it meets expectations and specification to the customer's satisfaction and that the customer will benefit from the project results after the project is over.

We can do this only by enticing the customer to meet with us, work with us, and talk to us.

Documenting Expectations

All our business communication becomes useful only when it is written down and when people agree to use the written documents and treat them as authoritative. We all like to believe that our memories are clear and that there was mutual understanding at meetings. The truth—revealed by psychological experiments and studies—is that even people regarded as having excellent memories often do not, in fact, remember things correctly. To avoid confusion, disappointment, and rework, put everything in writing.

In business, written agreements should replace memory.

The specification is the written statement of expectations. We should adhere to it and make sure that the customers understand that they will adhere to it as well. This is a strict rule, but we can present it in a very friendly way and be friendly and cooperative throughout the process. For example, adhering to the written specification doesn't mean it is set in stone. If, during the *doing stage,* a customer wants a change and we can do it and if we agree on a time and a price, then we agree, we change the written plan, and we deliver.

The specification is a living document. If done well, it will change little, but we can agree to change it.

Our ultimate goal is to provide the greatest value we can for the customer. We are strict not because we're selfish or we want to do less. We are strict because we understand that, to deliver any value at all, the project must succeed. And project management is risky. In doing communications management, we bring expectations under control, so that we can meet them and deliver customer delight.

Defining the Expectations Gap

Even when we have followed all the steps in Chapters 6 and 10 and what is written here, we have only specified the customers' expectations at the end of planning. Now, we have to keep expectations under management in the *doing stage.*

People tend to "remember" that they're going to get everything they want, even if they didn't ask for it. We also tend to dream of more things and somehow expect those to happen, as if by magic. While the customer's expectations are expanding, inflated by hopes and dreams, the specification isn't changing and actual results may be drifting downwards. While the customer is dreaming, the team is working, running into problems, and maybe dropping the ball here and there. Work quality results are likely to go down if we don't do anything to manage them. If we are not careful, this leads to a large gap, as illustrated in Figure 18-1, where the customer expects more than the specification and the team delivers less.

Dreams expand while results shrink.

If the project ends with expectations higher than the results, we have a disappointed customer—even if we deliver to specification. To prevent this, we

Figure 18-1. A project without gates allows an expectations gap

need more than just communication. We need clear, specific communication in a structured process. We create that by including the customer in each review gate.

Managing the Expectations Gap

The solution that manages expectations and results to prevent the expectation gap is gate reviews that bring the project up to specification while bringing the customer back down to earth, as shown in Figure 18-2.

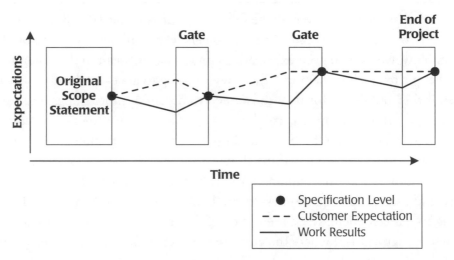

Figure 18-2. Managing expectations with gate reviews

In Figure 18-2, we show the two benefits of gate reviews. We use the gate to identify gaps between the specification and the work results. We then have the team improve the work results to meet the specification. At the same time, we bring the client to the gate review to get project status and see the product under development.

In the first gate in Figure 18-2, the client had some expectations that we understood as change requests, but rejected, bringing their expectations down to the specification. At the second gate, the client understood what kind of change request mattered. The client made a request—an increased expectation—and we approved the change request, increasing the specification to match the client's expectation. At the same time, we had the team do the work so that the results matched the new, higher specification. We then told the client that we couldn't afford any late changes to the project, so expectations stayed level to the end of the project. The work results dropped a little from the specification, but we fixed that in closing the project. As a result, we delivered not only to specification, but also to expectations.

Note that this process of ongoing, clear communication with the customer at gate reviews did more than eliminate the expectations gap. It also actually improved the specification and guided the team to deliver everything in the original specification and more. When the team members get to work effectively with the customers, they have a chance to do good work for people that they have actually met, which inspires them to do good work and deliver delight.

When we create gate reviews that include the customers, we must define the review to be appropriate. You don't want to overload customers with technical jargon until their eyes glaze over and they say, "OK, OK," just to escape. At the same time, you don't want to do a superficial job. Sort through the review milestones and decide which of the stakeholders should see what. You can refer to the communications plan, where you associated stakeholders with using—and therefore checking—different work packages. In addition, you should prepare appropriate presentations, which may include visuals or even physical prototypes for evaluation or testing.

Customers usually focus on one set of issues and the project team on another. Here is what most customers care about:

> ▶ *Benefits.* What will this do for me?

Gate reviews are a chance to stay in tune with your customer.

- *Features.* What has this got?
- *Usability.* How do I make this work? What do I do to get my work done or my satisfaction from this product or service?

Someone on the customer side will probably also be concerned about technical issues over the long haul such as installation, maintenance, compatibility, upgrading, disaster recovery, and replacement. Usually, we should meet with one customer representative separately on those issues.

At each gate review, the team is more likely to be concerned with these issues:

- *Components.* What's in here?
- *Requirements.* Does each thing work? Does it do what it's supposed to do?

Of course, there is a connection here. If the components meet the technical requirements and the technical requirements were designed to meet the functional specifications, then the product will be usable, with each feature working. If the product is easy to use and the features work, it will offer the benefits we planned. If it offers those benefits and we keep other expectations under management, then we will satisfy the customer.

I can't emphasize enough how important it is to meet expectations. You can do the best job in the world, but if the customers don't get what they expect, they will be disappointed. And each disappointed customer is one step toward a bad reputation—which is the last thing that a small business wants.

Ensure Communication with All Customers

So far, we've been talking as if the customer is just one person or as if all customers will want the same thing. Of course, that's not really true. So, now we need to talk about how to manage each customer's expectations and how to satisfy or delight each customer. There are two situations—one where we deliver a product to a group of customers and the other where we sell many products to many customers.

Managing Customer Expectations for a Group

In this case, the project might be a new computer system for a company or it might be a catered event, such as a wedding. If the target is a business customer, we need to address the expectations of three groups:

▶ *Executives* who want to make sure the results are valuable to the company.

▶ *Managers* who want to make sure that the department's work gets done, that the project doesn't interfere with routine work, and that, in the end, it will be easier, not harder, to work with the new system they will have when the project is done.

▶ *Workers* who want to know that their jobs will be easier with the new system.

Of course, in addition to these reasonable expectations that these people will have due to the goals of their jobs, people may also have personal preferences. We meet those when we can and manage them when we can't.

In addition to the customers, there may be other *stakeholders,* that is, other people who are affected by project results. We should maintain communications with all stakeholders.

How Much Money Are We Making?

One time, a computer consulting group designed and installed a customer relations management (CRM) system for a business client. CRM is a single system that supports marketing, sales, and customer service. The consulting group went to everyone in each of those departments, found out exactly what the old system did, found out exactly what they wanted, did a great job, and delivered everything.

The result was a disaster—because the consultants had missed a stakeholder. The old system generated one report that didn't go to anyone in marketing, sales, or customer service. That report was the *daily cash report* that went to the chief financial officer, showing him whether the company had made $1.5 million or only $500,000 that day. When they switched over to the new system, that report wasn't on his desk that day and he didn't know if the company was in the black so he could pay bills or in the red so that he had to borrow money that day.

The Lesson: Find every stakeholder, find what each one needs, and deliver it.

First, we specify their expectations into requirements. Then, in the *doing stage*, we keep them apprised of the progress of their particular requirements and include them in testing the product for the requirement they gave us. We make the product work for each stakeholder and get each stakeholder's approval. We can include this process in the gate review or, if it is a small item, we can work with the stakeholders whenever the components that concern them are done and ready for testing.

If we are doing a project for a group of consumers, then we will need to define the customer groups. For example, for a wedding we have the bride and groom, the bride's family, the groom's family, adult guests, child guests, and the celebrant (priest, pastor, rabbi, or judge). What will we do to delight each of them? Once we've defined who's who, we do the same process of expectation management as we would on any project.

Managing Customer Expectations for Individual Customers

If we are developing a product or service for sale, whether for businesses or consumers, then we can't meet all our customers during the project. The best we can do is to identify the customer groups related to this type of project and include sample customers or customer representatives—such as a marketing department—in the project. We should treat those groups like customers all the

Make a Customer Map

Take a look at your industry and the kind of projects you usually do. Write down answers to these questions:

▶ *Who are your customers?* Business or consumer? What kinds of companies and people?

▶ *Do you have just one customer per project or more than one?*

▶ *For each customer and stakeholder, what are their typical concerns?*

Once you write up your answers, you can create good marketing copy to sell your products and services by defining the benefits you offer. You can also create forms, templates, and checklists to make selling your services and doing your project work hassle-free.

The Lesson: Organize what you know about your customers to streamline projects and increase profit.

way through the project and work with them at each gate review. In addition, we should include advertising copy, product or service specifications, and customer instructions and guides as part of the project. When we do this, we can make sure that the specifications match the product and that reasonable interpretation of the advertising creates realistic expectations for future customers.

Conclusion: The Doing Is Done!

Congratulations! If you've taken a project this far through *Project Management for Small Business Made Easy*, then you've completed the doing stage. All that is left is to follow through to customer delight. You'll learn how in Chapters 19 and 20.

Chapter 19

Follow Through

I N *Chapters 19 and 20, you will learn to follow through, complet-*
ing the third and final stage of the project, and then deliver delight,
delivering the product and delighting the customer. First, we'll see why
the final stage of our project—when the customer gets the results—is
where, all too often, the stuff hits the fan. After looking at the challenges of following through on all types of projects, we'll examine the *follow-
through stage* at the three levels on which we manage on a project:

▶ *Technical follow-through,* which includes getting it done and getting
it right.

▶ *Project management follow-through,* which includes coordinating
with everyone, keeping track of everything, being ready for anything,
and writing down what we've learned.

▶ *Business follow-through,* which includes the steps we take to ensure
that the product is supported well and used well, so that value is realized, and then evaluating that value by comparing actual benefits
with the benefits we defined at the beginning of the project.

We'll consider the technical and project management levels in this chapter

It's All About Customer Value

Our project—our one-time, unique process—is about to deliver a product, service, or other result. If the specification was good and the customer uses the results well, then value will be realized. If we did good project work, then we are delivering good results on time and within the budget. But now is the time to make sure we're fully ready, we deliver and ensure product acceptance and valuable future use, and then we tie up all the loose ends to complete the project.

It doesn't work to deliver the product and run. Just like a golfer, batter, or tennis player focuses on what happens after hitting the ball, a project manager succeeds by focusing on what happens after the product is delivered. This is the secret of following through: focus on the customer, on delivering solutions and value, not just results and products, and the value will be realized.

That's what it really means to *get it done right!*

and the business level in the next chapter. At the end of these two chapters, you'll know how to follow through and deliver delight.

Our goal in project management and in small business is more than customer *satisfaction*; it's customer *delight*. Satisfied customer like what they get and walk away—and might never come back. The keys to success in small business are customer retention—that is, repeat business—and employee retention—that is, keeping our team members for the long term. When we achieve customer delight in our projects, we get both.

What is customer delight? We achieve customer delight when a customer says, "The product exceeded my expectations. More than that, I was delighted by every interaction I had with every person who works for the company."

Can you think of a company that delights you, that has done such excellent customer service that it's made you into a loyal customer? If so, then you know what I mean. If not, imagine how easy it would be to run your company if customers kept coming back, asking for more. When you learn the art of delivering customer delight from this chapter, you'll know how to make that happen, project after project, customer after customer.

How does customer delight help with repeat business and staff retention? Let's answer that in terms of the three types of projects: a project for a customer, a project to develop a new product, and a project to improve internal operations.

A project for a customer. When we deliver customer delight along with results, customers get exactly what they wanted. If it is a practical item—a business solution or a custom personal practical product—they know how to use it and realize value. If it is an item of beauty, they see its value. In addition, you gave them no hassles throughout the project. So, they'd be happy to use you again or refer you to their associates and friends. When a team delivers delight to customers, the members have reason to be happy. Being part of project success and working for appreciative customers is a good reason to stay right where they are, instead of leaving for another job.

A project to develop a new product. If we develop a new product that delivers customer delight, our company could be rolling in gold. We now have a product that will keep customers coming back. It's up to the production team to keep up the quality and the marketing and sales team to move the product, but we've made their jobs easy by giving them something that they can sell based on value. If they follow through, then the company's success will mean repeat customers and the production and marketing teams will have profitable, steady work. The project team can be rewarded through bonuses when the product exceeds expectations, as well as appreciation from the head of the company and the whole company.

A project to improve internal operations. If our project gives our employees a better way of working, then customer delight means that the people in affected departments are doing their jobs more easily and getting better results. If it's a profit center, then profits increase as their work gets easier, they have better information, and they can focus more on delighting *their* customers. If it's a cost center, then costs go down, corporate information improves, and profit margins go up. Employees are doing better jobs with less hassle, so they stay with the company. The company is paying more attention to the customers, so customers stay with the company.

So, now we know our goal. But it isn't easy to get there. If it were, then every company would do it and our country would be full of happy customers and employees working on good business systems without any hassle. Heck, we'd probably be down to a three-day workweek. We'd be so efficient that we could work less and enjoy life more with all those delightful products!

Well, life isn't like that—and there's a reason. Customers are people and people are unpredictable. They always want something new and different. Delighting them over and over is a real challenge. It means being able to deliver unique work and get it done right the first time. It also means getting better at what we do, project after project. If you want to keep getting better, set your sights on customer delight and read on to see what challenges you face and how to master them.

The Challenges of Following Through

What makes follow-through so difficult? Systems theory proposes an answer to that question. When we look at processes that occur in time, we can see two types. One type, which is easier, matches what we do in the *doing stage*. The other type of process, which is harder and full of unexpected events, is what happens in the *follow-through stage*.

> *When the product meets the customer, will they fall in love?*

The first is the unfolding of a plan in a known environment. Most of project work is like that. Once we have laid out our scope statement, we are working down into the details of planning, changing only very small things. The more we plan, the more our environment is set. When the plan is complete, we roll along a course we've set. We've even—as best we could—thought through the things that could take us off the path. In this way, following a plan and doing the work to make the plan unfold, we are doing our best to keep the unpredictable at bay. In systems terms, we've defined the project in its work environment as a system and we're trying not to interact with any new systems. We're just letting the work unfold.

All of that changes when we get to the *follow-through stage*. When we deliver the product, it encounters the customer. The product is one system and the customer is another. When two systems meet, they form a new system— and anything can happen. This is the second type of process that occurs in time: two systems meeting with unpredictable results. We see it all the time in art and in life: two people fall in love, but are they meant for each other? Will they keep delighting in each other? That's the basis of many romances, from *The Taming of the Shrew* to *Sleepless in Seattle*. What makes it so much fun is that it's unpredictable.

Well, we encounter that same situation at the end of a project, when the customer meets the product. Even if the customers got what they wanted, will it delight them? Will they use it, realize value, and come back for more? The problem is that what is exciting in drama is nerve-racking in reality, especially when the results of weeks or months of work depend on that unpredictable event—and even more when the future of our business hangs in the balance. What if it doesn't work for the customers?

In formal project management life cycles, the follow-through stage is called *transition to production*. One of my clients has an informal name for it—*the storm period*. The client is an IT development group delivering new computer systems to internal customers. The members of that group know from experience that they will be overwhelmed with lots of unpredictable problems during transition to production—like being caught out in a storm in a small sailboat. In this chapter, you'll learn how to bring your project through the storm and safely to port.

So, when two systems meet for the first time, unpredictable things happen. The first thing we can learn from this is that the issues that come up in the *follow-through stage* are fundamentally different from the issues that come up at any other time during the project. The second thing is that, if we think through the nature of the systems, we can probably identify the most common problems. Let's do that now, looking at the follow-through stage for projects for a customer, projects that develop a new product, and projects that change internal operations.

A project for a customer. First, we have to distinguish between two types of value the customer is expecting: useful value and enjoyment. In each case, the potential problems are different.

If the customer expects useful value, then the unpredictable element will usually arise from one of two areas. The first is barriers to effective, efficient use. If the system doesn't work right when the customer gets it, that's one cause of trouble. If the customer resists learning it or has trouble learning it well, that's another. Worst is when both of those are happening—the system isn't working and the people resist learning. In those cases, the product and the customer just don't come together in a useful way. We may have to do a full restart on delivery and training to make the project succeed. To prevent these problems, we should focus our attention on ensuring that the system works right at the customer location before the customers see it and on designing, promoting, and implementing an effective training program. The second set of storms comes if the customer is not integrated, that is, if the customer groups are divided, disagreeing about details of the goal. Here are some examples. If some users like it and others don't, we get partial acceptance, which can lead to little or no value. If the executives like it but the users don't, then we get paid but the customer realizes little value and doesn't come back. If the users like it but the executives don't, we might not get paid. If the customer can't support it and keep it running, then there is less value and the customer won't come back. We can work to prevent all of these problems by maintaining good communications with all stakeholders, resolving all open issues, and then making sure that satisfaction from any one group of customers is reported to all the other groups.

If the customer expects enjoyment, then the key is that the customer likes or loves the product or service *and doesn't feel irritated by any part of it at all.* A visit to a restaurant where the food was excellent but the wait was long leaves a memory of a long wait—and results in a lost customer. A bus tour of an exotic location with wonderful sights and events but no air conditioning on the bus is a miserable vacation. So, the key is to focus on the customer's experience of the product or service down to the last detail. In addition, we have to ensure that we are ready for anything, that we can respond effectively to any reasonable customer request. This requires contingency planning and a good support team.

A project that develops a new product. In this case the storm period can be relatively mild if we work closely with the teams that will produce, support, and sell the new product after the project is over. These are your first customers. All these people are within our company, so we can have good access to them. The biggest challenges arise when a company is so compartmentalized or those people are so busy that you don't get to work with them throughout the project—or at least in planning and a lot near the end. If they can tell you their concerns, then you can plan for and prevent many problems. When you do, you are designing quality into the product from the very beginning. Products that are easy to produce, have low maintenance costs, and are easy to market have large profit margins. Our best approach here is, from the beginning of our project, to define quality as that which delivers the product with the best features and fewest hassles to the production, marketing, and maintenance teams of our company.

A project that changes internal operations. Key issues in this type of project are a lack of customer involvement in design specification, so that the system is not easy to use; customer resistance to learning and using the new system; a technical failure of the new system in the production environment; and a conflict between learning the new system and doing regular work. Our best approach is to work cooperatively with the internal customer team. We work to include the customers from the beginning, promote the new system's value, listen to the resistance, and deal with any genuine issues. We make sure the system works in the production environment before the customers see it. We define the priority of training in effective and efficient use of the new system for the actual work and we schedule time for it.

Now that we have an outline of the issues for each type of project, let's look at the work of the follow-through stage in managing the technical level, the project level, and the business level of the project as we deliver the product and make sure we *get it done right!*

Technical Follow-Through

Technical follow-through is very simple:

- ▶ We complete scope, getting it ready.
- ▶ We ensure quality, getting it right.

There are two things we can do to make this a success. First, we can do extra work to ensure that the specification really delivers what the customer wants. Second, we can do extra work and testing to ensure that the product meets its specifications and performs as required.

Ensuring a Good Specification

In ensuring a good specification, we must address two issues: ensuring a good customer specification, so that the customer can use the product well, and ensuring a good fit of the product into the production environment.

There are two approaches to ensuring a good customer specification. We covered one of them in Chapters 6 and 10, where you learned how to do requirements elicitation by sharing a picture or sample of the product, getting feedback, and creating the document specification. This is a good approach, but when the customer is going to use the product and that use requires that they really understand it well, we may need to do more. For those situations, our best solution is to develop an early working version called a *prototype,* and testing the prototype with the customer throughout the project. This way, some of the customer users—maybe all of them—get to interact with and improve the product. By the end of the project, they like it because they've made it work for themselves. We can adjust our project plan to include customer prototype testing and feedback in one of two ways. One approach is to insert more gate reviews that include the customer. The other is to have a customer worker assigned to the team, either part time or full time, to keep testing and using each component as the team develops it. Both of these methods are commonly used in software development when a custom system is being built to improve the way a department works.

The second issue is to make sure that the product will work in the customer environment. The key here is to get to know the environment really well from all architectural and engineering perspectives. Here are samples of questions we should ask:

- What are the environmental factors, such as temperature and humidity, that might cause the product to fail?

- What resources are we assuming the customer has, such as space for the product, electricity, and so forth? Do they meet the specific requirements of our product? I've seen new air conditioners and refrigerators purchased that couldn't be plugged in because the outlet was the wrong voltage or the appliances constantly tripped the circuit breaker.

- Have we identified every user? Do we know how each one will use the new product and what he or she expects?

- Have we identified every type of maintenance, support, and training related to the new system, now and in the future? Does everyone responsible for maintaining and supporting the system and for learning or teaching know how to do their work, so that the system will work effectively and efficiently for its intended purpose throughout its production life? Have we ensured that they will be able to do that for the life of the product?

- Have we identified every stakeholder and kept in touch with them all, so that we know what each expects?

- Have we asked stakeholders to triple-check that the environment and environmental requirements have not changed since they were specified during project planning?

Using these questions will be very different for different types of products, services, and solutions with different types of customers. Within our own industry, we should develop effective checklists to make sure we *get it done right!*

Ensuring That We Meet the Specification

If our specification is good, our next step is to ensure that the product conforms to all specifications—the work of quality engineering. We have already discussed this at length in Chapter 16: Quality, Eliminate Error. Tracing all requirements from customer to components and through the test plan, test design, testing, and confirmation of corrective action and retesting is essential. This approach links benefits to features to component specifications. A project full of checklists will succeed—if they are used with a focus on quality. We need to make sure the team members are not so pressured to get it done on time that they don't get it done right.

As we approach the final gate, additional tests are required. All of the different types of tests for all different industries would fill a book thicker than this one. But we want to make sure that the product will work into the future, not just when we deliver it.

Test design is difficult. How can we say that, because a product passed a test, it will work in the real world? Here are some questions we should consider when designing tests.

> *Is it done? Is it done right?*

> *When it passes the tests and fails in reality, we fail the ultimate test: we lose the customer.*

- ▶ Can we design a test where the system is working in the real production environment, as close as possible, doing what it is intended to do?
- ▶ Can we include customers in our tests?
- ▶ Can we design stress tests that test the system at capacity and over?
- ▶ Can we design aging tests that show how the system will work in the future?
- ▶ Can we test how the system will work after it receives routine maintenance? After a failure, emergency shutdown, and restart?
- ▶ Can we test maintenance and emergency procedures performed by the customer support team?

This list could go on and on. It's a tough world out there and we need to do a lot to make sure our product will keep producing long after we deliver it.

Testing, Testing: Going Around in Circles

We must allow time for testing, rework, and retesting to ensure that each module and the whole product pass all tests. The closer we get to our delivery date, the harder this is to do. Just as we're running out of time, we have more and more completed components to test.

If we don't leave time for fixing after testing, we deliver defects.

We have to assume that some components will fail in testing and that the product will fail some tests, too. Of course, we don't know which ones will fail; if we did, we'd fix them before they failed. So, if we don't know what the failures will be, how do we know how much time to leave for the tests? There is a rule of thumb that might help. Calculate the time that it will take—in hours of effort—to test everything and verify it as if it will pass all tests. Then multiply by 3.2. So, if testing will take 10 hours if nothing goes wrong, allow 32 hours for that test series. Until you develop a track record of your own, that is a good place to start.

We've now completed our guide to managing the technical level during follow-through to make sure the specification is right and the product meets the specification. The product is as ready as it can be. Are we? Is the team? Is the customer? We'll face those challenges in the next section.

Project Management Follow-Through

In this section, we look at how to do good project management in the follow-through stage. We want to prepare as much as we can for the unpredictable as the following things happen:

- The product, service, or solution starts to operate in the real world.
- The customer learns to use and starts using the product, service, or solution.
- The customer starts to maintain and support the product.
- The customer executives react to the end of the project and receipt of the product.

Does everyone have everything he or she needs?

As our team is finishing up and testing the product, getting it ready for delivery, we should turn our attention to these essentials:

- Coordinate with everyone.
- Keep track of everything.
- Be ready for anything.

177

If we do all of that, we will be as ready as we can be to do good follow-through. Let's look at each in turn.

Coordinate with Everyone

I hope you haven't thrown your communications plan into a drawer and forgotten about it. If you have, get it out and dust it off well before your delivery date.

Now is the time to triple-check everything with everyone. Review your list of stakeholders and their concerns. Call up or meet with each one and make sure that they are all satisfied with all that they have heard and seen. Ask what you need to do to make delivery day a success for them and for everyone involved with the customer.

Then follow through. Every time a stakeholder requests something, write it down and make sure you or a team member takes care of it and lets the stakeholder know it was done. If you need a stakeholder to do something for you, ask—then put it in writing and keep bugging him or her until you get what you need. You want good communications feedback and good action feedback on everything the project needs. Your team is probably used to that by now. But your customers are not. So, ask for what you need—and keep asking until you get it. I'm assuring you, and you should assure them, that the only way to ensure successful product delivery is if everyone triple-checks the completion of every little detail.

Keep Track of Everything

It's not enough just to talk with everyone; we also have to keep track of everything. At www.qualitytechnology.com/DoneRight, there is a tool I call the Open Issues Template. It covers all the different types of information we have to track to get through any project in the follow-through stage. It's also good for any project in crisis. Here are the lists of the types of issues you need to track—and what can happen if you don't:

- ▶ *Decisions to be made.* If we leave a decision unmade, someone will be disappointed. For example, if a change request came in and we lose track of it, someone will expect to be getting something, but it won't be in the specification.
- ▶ *Recently resolved decisions.* We keep these on the list because we need to tell everyone what the decision was. If someone isn't told, then he or she won't be on the same page. Have you ever missed a

meeting because no one told you that the location had changed?

▶ *Work to be done.* These are the simple, straightforward items. If a piece of work isn't done, then some part of the product won't be delivered. Wrap up the loose ends and deliver to avoid customer dissatisfaction.

▶ *Problems to be solved.* Problems are more complicated than work. With work, we know what has to be done and how long it will take. But when we discover a problem, we know only the symptom. We still need to diagnose and define the problem, then work on a solution, and finally retest. Unresolved problems near the end of a project are crucial. They require attention from us and from our team. Make sure each one is assigned to someone and resolved.

▶ *Documents to be changed.* Have you ever bought a consumer electronics item or tool and found that the picture in the instructions doesn't match what you bought? That happens when instructions or other documentation isn't updated with the changes to the product. Track all needed changes to all documents within the project and all deliverable documents.

▶ *Information to be gathered.* Here, someone knows something, but someone else needs to know it. We find the information and deliver it to the person who needs it, so the job can get done. Imagine blowing an installation day because you or someone on your team gets lost on the way to the customer's office. Define everything anyone needs to know and get the information to each person well in advance.

If we've taken care of this situation, all of the issues are named. That leaves two problems. We have to resolve the issues. We also have to be ready for the issues that we haven't heard about—and maybe never even imagined.

Be Ready for Anything

Can you imagine the afternoon sun ruining your day? For a TV producer, that's quite possible. Matt Williams, a TV producer who makes commercials, tells a story that illustrates what it means to be ready for anything on a project.

A crew was shooting a scene indoors. It was running a bit behind, but not much. The current scene had to be finished before 1:30 p.m., because at that point the sun would come through the window, the lighting would change, and the scene would look totally different. The person responsible for lighting had two options. He could either count on the scene being done on time or ask the props crew to build a big wooden overhang to put outside to shade the window. There were a lot of things going on that day, he was counting on the crew not to fall further behind, and he didn't ask the props team to prepare an overhang.

He was wrong. Just before 1:30, the person responsible for lighting said that they'd need to stop shooting until a shade could be built. The producer was mad, because it pushed the filming closer and closer to very expensive overtime. The props team was mad because they had to do it at the last minute, when they could have had it ready in advance. One poor decision on a shooting day threw everyone off and it could have been very expensive.

Project delivery days are like shooting days, so we should learn from folks who make films. Matt tells me that the key to success in the TV and movie industry is to have four or five solutions for every problem that might come up and to be ready to decide which one is best in under 30 seconds and then turn everything upside down to make it work. Folks in the film industry get a lot of practice thinking and working that way.

In one sense, project management is even harder. We don't have to work that way very often. Most of the time, most of the project is under our control. But, at the crucial moment, delivery day, all that changes. We have to be ready for anything—and all the work we did up to that point may depend on what we do in that one critical moment.

Project delivery takes many different forms, so our preparation has to take many forms, as well.

- ▶ *We ship a product to a customer.* Will they be able to install it, understand it, and use it without us?

- ▶ *We install the product for them and leave them to use it.* Will they be able to understand it and use it without us?

When There's No Tomorrow

Project managers can learn a lot from event planners who do conferences, weddings, and other one-time events. Of course, to do that kind of work, you need to know your stuff. But there is also a certain skill of visualization, an ability to see what will happen, in order to arrange things right, that is very useful for anyone who does a lot of preparatory work in the hopes of delighting a customer.

The Lesson: Learn to visualize the event, picture how it can go wrong, picture how it can go right, and then make sure it goes right.

▶ *We provide installation, training, and support.* Will everything go well during installation and training? Will all the people involved work well together? Will they come to the training and be able to use the solution productively?

▶ *We deliver to many locations, either for one customer or for many customers.* In this case, we need to make sure that each delivery, with appropriate installation and training, is a well-planned mini-project.

▶ *We provide a service, supporting a one-time event.* Here, all the value is at the delivery time. There is no second chance. A wedding planner can't say, "I'm sorry I forgot the cake and flowers. Could you get married again next week?"

▶ *We provide a solution and the customer isn't even there.* We might be fixing a broken pipe while the customer is away. We have to do good work with little guidance and then follow up with the customer.

▶ *We work directly with the customer's customer.* Here, we represent the customer: if our team makes a mistake, it makes the customer look bad. For example, we might be doing an advertising mailing for the customer. We have to more than triple-check the quality of everything we do, ensure successful delivery, and follow up with the customer.

What is your situation? Whatever it is, here are the keys to successful follow-through:

▶ *Know your field.* Many of the situations described above are routine for professionals in specific fields.

▶ *Plan delivery day as a subproject.* Make a detailed plan and timeline of activities to prepare, do, and follow through on delivery day. Check scope, time, cost, quality, risk, the team, and all the other areas. Then check them again. Then be ready for problems you never even imagined.

If we prepare well, delivery day is exciting. It's a chance to see all of our work pay off. If we don't get fully ready, then we'll have a really lousy time and our customer and we will pay a steep price. Either we'll need to do a lot of rework and follow-up or the return on investment for the whole project will be reduced or lost altogether.

When It's up to the Customer

When we ship products to customers or they buy them and take them home to assemble or install, then their delight with us depends on their own ability to put together the product and make it work. That is why good companies spend lots of money on careful design of simple, glossy, graphical instruction sheets that are supposed to be easy to use. Think of something you bought that could have been difficult to set up, but had really good instructions. Now, imagine that you are the project manager. What design skills and testing went into making those instructions work? You can bet the instructions were a defined deliverable at the beginning of the project, not thrown together at the last minute.

The Lesson: We want to include instructions and documentation as deliverables in our initial plan and test them along with the product.

Conclusion: Safely Ashore!

You've now learned how to take your project through the *follow-through stage* at the technical and project levels. If your project has come this far, your sailboat is safely in the harbor and the cargo has been offloaded into the customer's warehouse. We're almost done. But we need to do follow-through at the business level to ensure complete project success, as you will learn in Chapter 20, Deliver Delight.

Chapter 20

Deliver Delight

N OW, WE MOVE BEYOND THE REALM MOST PROJECT MANAGERS work in, into an opportunity to really boost our business. Using techniques developed in Total Quality Management, we use each contact with our customers to help them be delighted with us. All through the book, we've talked about hassle-free work. Now, we'll try to take that to the next level: hassle-free business.

It isn't easy, because we can't train our customers the way we can train our team. But it pays off. Why? Because a small company with loyal customers has less hassle, higher total income, and higher net revenue. We may end up with more clients than we can handle, in which case we get a choice: we can grow or we can stay small and do only work we love to do for clients who are a delight to work with.

This chapter includes two techniques for ensuring customer delight on each project and a summary of all that you've learned that will truly make project management easy for you:

▶ *Business follow-through* shows you how to ensure customer delight.

▶ *Follow-up after the project* shows you how to be sure the customer realizes value and how to learn lessons so that you and your team get better at what you do, project after project.

▶ *All you need to know* summarizes what you've learned in 20 steps to project success plus five paths to project disaster you can be sure to avoid!

Business Follow-Through

To follow through at the business level, we need to be attentive to customer needs; to take care of loose ends for the customer, the team, and our own company; and to check the project results against the goal that we defined at the beginning when we defined the value and benefits of doing the project.

Is the Customer Delighted?

How do we know if the customers are delighted? We ask. And, in asking, either we increase their delight by showing, once more, that we care or we have a chance to make up for any problems. And, if we are given that chance, we should use it to the fullest. Be sure to take care of any final commitments that you make.

If you are the customer, you need to talk to yourself. Are you delighted with the results of the project? Are you using the new product, service, or solution you created? Are you realizing value? If not, why not? In a small business, it is all too easy to get caught up with the next thing and the next and not use the good work we've done. But what we don't use has no value for us.

If we have a single customer or customer group—inside our company or external—we should meet with them to hear whatever they need to get closure and ensure project success and lasting value. You might prepare a questionnaire or meeting agenda based on the original project plan, to ask your customers if they are getting what they need. If they are external, that is also a good time to ask about the possibility of repeat business or to get a reference or a referral.

If we delivered results to many customers, then we should include some kind of survey or evaluation in our project plan so that we can know what they thought of our work and our service. When distributing surveys widely, it pays to provide some kind of incentive or bonus for replies, so that we get lots of feedback.

However we ask the customers if they were delighted, we should follow through on the answer:

▶ *If customers are delighted, approach them appropriately about the possibility of repeat business, references, and referrals.* If you are not comfortable doing this, check out books on networking as a marketing technique—it can really build your business.

▶ *If customers are generally appreciative but have some concerns, listen and follow through.* For those that cannot be resolved, show the customers that you understand the problems and promise that you will make a change to do better next time. Do that even if you expect never to work with those customers again. That promise is really to yourself as a professional—a promise to learn lessons and get better at what you do. If you can address the customers' problems, do so. At the end of a project, it pays to go the extra mile to create lasting appreciation and earn repeat business.

▶ *If customers have a major complaint, work out a fair resolution.* Do what you can within reason to come to a good resolution. Don't give away the store, but if there is some reasonable extra or discount you can offer, then do so. Showing customers that you are very concerned to deliver satisfaction even when you can't goes a long way to building a relationship. It also is an excellent way to prevent bad publicity and even more unfortunate circumstances, such as legal action.

Don't just listen to your customer. Listen, then respond!

Know where you stand on delivering customer delight. Keep learning until you are doing it project after project. There is no more delightful path to small business success than a long line of delighted customers.

Are All the Loose Ends Tied Up?

The Project Management Institute has two processes in the Closing process group: Close Project and Contract Closure.

Close Project is a very general instruction to close all activities in all processes from all process groups. We can do this by reviewing our project plan. We check with everyone that each task is done and we double-check with the customers to see that they got everything they wanted. Then we review the project, walking through all nine of the knowledge areas, and we tie up any loose ends.

Wrap up your project in a tight package.

Contract Closure is an additional step whenever there was a contract as part of the project work. This includes both contracts where we are the performing party and we delivered something to a customer and contracts

Service Recovery: Exceed Expectations

When we make a mistake, we have a chance to make a customer for life. To see what I mean, try this out. Remember three times you were a customer, one for each of these situations.

▶ You got what you paid for, no more and no less.
▶ You didn't get what you paid for. You complained and got what you paid for, but no compensation.
▶ You didn't get what you paid for. You complained and got what you paid for, an apology, and more as well.

Which of these companies would you use again and recommend to others? If you're like me and most people I know, the company that makes a mistake then makes it right with bells on wins your heart.

You can learn that approach and use it. It's called *service recovery*. My friend Jim Rooney teaches about service recovery through his company, People Smart Tools. (There's a link to his site at my site, www.qualitytechnology.com/DoneRight.)

This four-step method for service recovery is adapted from Jim's newsletter, *The People Smart Toolbox*. Jim tells a story of a server who handled an error made at a restaurant.

"Here is what the server did right:

1. He acknowledged that there was a mistake without placing blame.
2. He quickly resolved our complaint.
3. He was truly interested in making our experience pleasant.
4. He offered a gift of appeasement.

"What system do you have in place for service recovery excellence in your organization? Send an e-mail to your staff and ask them to develop ideas for exceeding the customer's expectations when bad service is received.

"Your employees will provide good ideas that you haven't considered. Take those ideas and formulate them into an 'official protocol' for your business. Introduce the ideas and the training (role-playing is a must) with the specific intent of creating customer advocates for your organization.

"Every business or organization—medical arts, professional service providers, business-to-business operations, retail, manufacturing, real estate, automotive services, nonprofit organizations and government—can benefit from a proactive attitude of service recovery."

The Lesson: When you make a mistake, grow a relationship that can withstand mistakes using service recovery.

where we received something from a vendor or consultant. We make sure that the final invoice is sent, received, and paid. We also send any appropriate legal documents that sign off on the fact that the contract is complete, giving the date and stating whether all terms were met or if anything still needs to be resolved. If anything needs to be resolved, we schedule or delegate appropriate action.

As the last step of the project, we should look at unresolved issues outside the project. What work has fallen behind while we were busy getting this project done? What will our team do next? What do we want to do to thank our team, our vendors, our customers, and other stakeholders? How do we want to celebrate?

Follow-up After the Project

There are two things we can do after the project is over. One is for the customer and the other is for the project team. The post-project business review ensures customer value after the customer has been using the product, service, or results of the project for a while. The lessons-learned process helps the team do better projects next time.

The Post-Project Business Review: Is Value Realized?

At the end, we should look back to where we started. We began this project with a purpose, a reason *why* we were doing this project. We defined value, defined what we would need to deliver and how it would need to be used to receive that value. We also said that that value would arise from certain specific benefits and that those benefits would come from product features.

We now need to return to the original project charter or initial plan and ask, "Did we do what we said we were going to do? Did we solve that problem or realize that opportunity? Was it as successful as we had hoped it would be? Did we hit our target? Was the value realized? Are the benefits there? Did the features work and keep working?"

In some cases, we can answer those questions shortly after the project is over. Here are some examples:

▶ *We delivered a project for a customer.* We succeeded if they paid the bill, expressed satisfaction or delight, and came back with repeat business or provided references or referrals.

187

▶ *We ran a one-time event*, such as a presentation and booth at an annual industry conference. We defined certain goals in advance, such as getting a certain number of inquiries and selling a certain dollar value in products. We can compare our actual results with our goals. If we didn't reach them, we may be able to define some follow-up actions that will help close the gap.

On some projects it will take some time to see if we are going to realize value. The day the project delivers may be the beginning of realizing value, but it may take years to realize the full value. In that case, we should arrange for a follow-up analysis at an appropriate time. Here are two examples of that type of project:

▶ *We bring a new product to market.* It will take time to see if the product meets the expectations of our sales forecasts for its product life cycle and if its production and maintenance costs will be as low as we expected.

▶ *We launch an advertising campaign.* It will take some time to see if it brings us new business.

At the appropriate time, we check to see if value was realized. We compare what the customer is doing now and two things: our project plan for features and benefits and what the customer was doing before the project started. If the customer is better off, value is realized. If we can measure that, for example, as a change in net revenue due to new product sales, that's great. If value is not realized, we should ask three questions:

▶ *Did we pick the right project?* Sometimes, we have a bright idea and we make it real, only to discover that it doesn't work in the marketplace or for the business.

▶ *Did we estimate well?* If the project cost more and took longer than originally planned, we should learn something from that. If project work was good, we can become better estimators so we estimate future projects more accurately. If project work was weak—as we can see in our lessons learned—then we can do better so that we deliver on time and on budget in the future.

▶ *Did we deliver what we planned?* Perhaps the reason value wasn't realized is that we did not deliver to specification. Learn why that happened and figure out how to do better next time.

What Will You Do Next?

After the project is over, be sure there's a bit of a celebration and a lot of appreciation. Don't just run right to the next thing.

Then ask yourself, "What will my team and I do next?" Is it back to routine work or is it on to the next project? Work schedules can get a little skewed during the storm period, so take some time to see how the business is doing. Find out what your business really needs and take care of what needs attention.

The Lessons-Learned Process

When we've delivered and done all we can for the customer, there is one more job to do for our own company and the project team. Every project is a unique chance to learn. We can turn expertise into experience by taking information from the project and developing two documents for future use:

▶ *Historical information*, including the project plan in all its stages and records of actual results, is useful for planning future projects. If we capture this information in an organized way and make it available, we are building our *organizational process assets*—our knowledge about how to do good projects.

▶ *Lessons learned* is a document that we can create at the end of any stage and also at the end of a project, saying what we have learned about how to get it done right. We can establish new guidelines, improve templates and tools, and define how we can become better project managers.

For a lessons-learned survey, check out www.qualitytechnology.com/DoneRight.

All You Need to Know

Repeat successes. Change your process after failures.

Now that you have learned a tremendous amount about good project management, it makes sense to focus on the most important points. We start with the top-20 list of points to make a project succeed. Then we look at five ways to get it wrong. By the end of this section, you'll not only know how to *get it done right*, but also know how to avoid the pitfalls that keep you from getting the project done at all.

The Top-20 List

Twenty items may seem like a lot, but I've grouped them in six short lists: one for planning the project, one for preparing your team, one for applying the nine knowledge areas, one for doing, one for using stages and gates, and one for following through.

Four key planning points:

1. *Do the right project.* Choose the project that gives you the biggest value for your effort and is most aligned with your company's strategy, moving you in the direction you want to go.

2. *Define scope clearly and precisely.*

3. *Plan the whole project.* Make a plan for each of the nine areas.

4. *Do good design.* Work with words and pictures to bring people with different perspectives onto the same page, contributing to and committed to the project.

Prepare your team in just two steps:

5. *Get the right team.* Using the WBS, define the skills needed and get people with those skills. Be honest about gaps and close them by taking time to learn to get it done right.

6. *Get the expertise you need.* Know that being expert in one area means not being expert in other areas—sometimes closely related disciplines. Recognize that projects, being unique work, require learning from and collaborating with experts. Remember: hiring experts you can work with is less expensive than *not* hiring experts you can work with.

Cover all the bases with the nine knowledge areas:

7. *Scope.* Define scope clearly. Teach the cost of changes, in order to reduce change requests. Then, manage all changes, adding to the project only when it is essential.

8. *Time and cost.* Use unbiased, accurate estimation techniques. Set up systems to gather, track, and analyze time and cost information, so you can keep time and cost under control

9. *Quality.* Focus on quality at all three levels to ensure value. At the technical level, trace requirements and design checking and testing throughout the project to reduce errors. Then design a test bed and implement the tests.

At the project level, work to prevent error; then find and eliminate any errors that slipped through. Do as much testing as you can as early as you can. Allow time for rework and retesting to ensure you've eliminated errors without letting new ones creep in. At the business level, include customers in testing and remember that the goals are customer delight and added value.

10. *Risk*. Plan for uncertainty; prepare for the unexpected. Perform risk management with your team every week of the project.

11. *Human resources*. Help each team member step up in self-management and technical expertise. Teach them all PDCA so that they can improve. Then teach them to work together, until you have a great team of great people.

12. *Procurement*. Get the supplies and resources you need. If your project involves contracts, be sure to keep the contracts in alignment with project value and specifications, not just generally associated with goals and work.

13. *Communications*. Make a communications plan and then follow it so that you are in touch with all stakeholders throughout the project. Make sure that all of them know what they need to know to make decisions and get work done. Analyze status information to create status reports. Be prompt and decisive.

14. *Integration*. Constantly direct corrective action. Evaluate all events that could change the project schedule and all scope change requests. Review the effects of any change on all nine areas before making a decision. Then implement a revised plan with rebaselining.

Keep the project on track with stages and gates:

15. *Use a life cycle*. At a minimum, put a gate at the beginning to clearly launch the project and then a gate after planning, a gate after doing, and a gate after following through.

16. *Make every gate a real evaluation*. Bring every deliverable—parts of the product, product documentation, technical documents, and the project plan and supporting documents—up to specification. If a project can't deliver value, be willing to cancel it.

Use feedback with your team and focus on scope and quality in the *doing stage*:

17. Use *feedback at all four levels*. Teach workers to stay on track and on schedule, ensure delivery of milestones, manage project risk, and manage

project change. Watch out for continuing problems that indicate a serious planning error, such as lack of attention to one of the nine areas or a poor architectural decision.

18. *Focus on scope and quality.* Get it all done and get each piece done right.

Follow through to success:

19. *Deliver customer delight.* Seek to exceed customer expectations and leave customers delighted with every encounter with your team. Use every success and every error as a chance to learn to do a better job.

20. *Remember value and lessons learned.* Compare actual value against planned value, so you can be honest about the degree of your success. Compile project historical information and lessons learned to make future projects easier.

Five Ways to Project Disaster

Success is a matter of moving ahead and steering clear of failure. Here are five fast tracks to failure, so that you can avoid them.

Five ways to *get it done wrong or not at all!*

1. *Don't think Scope-less is hopeless.* Don't decide what you are doing—just throw money at a problem.
2. *Focus on time and cost, not quality.* Get it done yesterday. Never let anyone spend money. Don't waste time checking anything—just get it done.
3. *Know the right thing to do.* Don't analyze problems. Don't listen to experts. And—absolutely, above all, whatever you do—be sure to ignore the customer. You wouldn't launch a project if you didn't know everything. What does anyone else know?
4. *Don't thank the team; just push them harder.* Don't waste time with planning. People ought to know what to do. Just tell the team to get it done now—or else.
5. *Avoid big problems.* All of our projects fail. And we've got no time for them, either—we're too busy putting out fires.

Is that a list of how to fail at projects? Or is it also a description of how all too many companies are run these days?

Conclusion: Success and Delight

Customer delight is a delightful goal. The journey toward it can be long, but the value lies in the journey. Each finished project, each satisfied customer, and even each lesson learned from a mistake or a failure is a step in the right direction. Learn the lessons of good follow-through and you do more than master project management: you master good customer service and excel at growing your business.

You have a chance to be different. Differentiate yourself from the competition, boost your business, make work fun for you and your team, and delight your customers by applying what you've learned in *Project Management for Small Business Made Easy.*

We can learn from the successes of others. In Chapter 21, Know What You Want, Plan, and Go for It, you'll learn how an excellent entrepreneur and natural project manager has launched four successful businesses in just a few years. All of them delight customers and do very well indeed. In Chapter 22, Planning a Year of Projects, you'll learn how I plan projects that will grow my business every year and also how I teach my clients to plan growth.

Last, in Appendix A, Forms and Tools, you'll get a big boost. The quick and easy way to learn a new system is with tools and templates. Templates are forms that make sure you ask all the right questions, check everything, and keep things moving throughout the project. There are even more templates at my web site, www.qualitytechnology.com/DoneRight.

Chapter 21

Storefront Success: Know What You Want, Plan, and Go for It

THIS CASE STUDY IS THE STORY OF A NATURAL PROJECT MANAGER. Paul Manning has never studied project management. I'm not sure he even knew it was a separate field of business expertise until I dropped by for a cappuccino at The Front Porch Café in Kill Devil Hills on North Carolina's Outer Banks and we got to talking. When I met him, he and his wife Susannah Sakal had already opened three successful stores right next to each other—The Front Porch Café, home of "the best coffee on the Outer Banks" for three years running according to readers of *The Coast* magazine; Glazin' Go Nuts, a paint-your-own pottery store; and the Garden of Beadin', a bead shop. In the last six months, they've opened The Front Porch Café Nags Head, five miles away.

Paul took his time planning and preparing to launch his new businesses. That preparation paid off, as all four stores are doing well. More important:

▶ Paul and Susannah are realizing their dreams, growing and learning.

▶ They are providing opportunities for their staff to learn and grow.

▸ The café is a vibrant part of the local community.

Paul has not done everything right, it hasn't always been easy, and he'll be the first to tell you that it's been a lot of work. But, because he did the important things right—having a clear concept, values, and goal, and doing good planning and architecture—the years have been enjoyable instead of overly stressful. Let's take a look at what he's done and, more important, how he did it.

A Long Time Coming: Opening the First Store

Paul and Susannah took the first step of turning their dream into a reality in 1993, when they wrote a business plan for The Front Porch Café. In 1996, they took the next step by moving to the Outer Banks, the region of the North Carolina shore where they wanted their new store. They had saved up some money to launch the business and were getting to know the local community and changing their lifestyle to be ready to open the store. The opportunity came when the national company Paul worked for was sold and Paul didn't see eye to eye with the new owners. They wanted to boost the stock value and sell the company, instead of continuing to invest in long-term value. Paul decided it was time to make the big jump from employee to self-employed business owner.

Then he and Susannah spent over six months scouting for the right location. As Paul says about a storefront consumer business, "You have to find the right location. That's where you put your nest egg."

Lesson #1: Start-up success is about careful planning that lets us feel the right moment when it comes and know that it's time to take the leap.

The Front Porch Café is guided by two simple principles:

▸ *Exceptional customer service.* The folks at Front Porch try to know every customer by name and know his or her regular drink. One time, a regular parked his car right out front and Susannah saw him and prepared his coffee the way he liked it, a latte with two sugars and whole milk. He was chatting on the cell phone, so she brought it out to him. He told his friend, "You won't believe this. I'm sitting in front of The Front Porch Café, and they brought me my coffee before I even got out of the car."

See Chapter 4 for more on turning your dream into a business.

195

▶ *High-quality coffee, teas, and other items.* As you'll see, Paul has paid a great deal of attention to making sure that he serves consistently excellent beverages and food to his customers.

Paul points out that the coffee shop experience can vary widely. Some places focus on fast service, low price, a neighborhood feel, or a wide selection of items. Any of these could work—as long as they work for the entrepreneur.

Lesson #2: For entrepreneurial success, define what makes you unique and express that in your business.

See Chapter 2 to figure out which projects work best for your unique business.

In the first four or five months, either Paul or Susannah was always there. During that time, they developed their team. When team members were showing the same attentive customer service that the owners had, it was time to let them take over some shifts. Over time, people who have stayed on year-round have moved up into management, opening the door for Paul and Susannah to focus on other parts of the business.

See Chapter 10 to build the team for your company or your project.

Lesson #3: Nothing can replace your own time and attention to your store. You are essential.

Lesson #4: Find good people who want a career with you and help them grow.

Gaining, Training, and Retaining Staff

Like most owners of customer-service oriented business, Paul finds that getting and keeping the right people is one of the toughest ongoing challenges to the business. In addition, his business is seasonal, so he needs to pick up new employees every summer.

Paul is lucky in that he gets enough applicants. Students come in to apply for jobs as summer approaches. Paul says that, most of the time, he can decide if the person is a good fit within the first ten minutes. If applicants seem friendly and outgoing, attentive to others, and willing to learn, help, and get along, then they are good candidates. He generally hires on the spot. He does take references and sometimes checks them, but that rarely reverses his decision. New employees are told that they need to show that they are doing well after the first week and that a final decision will be made at the end of the first month.

New employees are paired with experienced employees, doing the same job on the same schedule in an informal mentoring program. They learn the job by osmosis, supported by formal training. In addition, there is an employee manual that includes not only the rules, but also the spirit and attitude of the Café. One of the rules, for instance, is that the customer always comes first. At the Café, if your boss just asked you to do something and then you see a customer, you set aside the job you were given and take care of the customer first.

New employees are given feedback and guidance. For instance, one young woman seemed very outgoing during the interview, but once she started work, it was as if she was a different person. She was quiet and didn't step up to help people. Paul let her know that that would need to change. When it didn't, she was let go at the end of the month.

Paul's decision to make the trial period one month long is based on several ideas. One is that a person can learn the job in a week, but it takes about a month to see if he or she is fitting in with the job, the team, the Café, and the customers. Another reason for deciding at the end of the first month is that, if you let a person go after only a month, you are generally not liable for unemployment. If you want to terminate someone after three or four months, you will probably be liable for some unemployment unless the person is clearly breaking the rules—stealing or not showing up for work. So Paul has decided that it is best to make a clear decision at the end of the first month.

Paul says that the team is very good at seeing if a person fits in and he checks with the other team members at the end of an employee's first month to see if they think he or she should stay or leave. Including the long-term team members in these decisions also builds their confidence in being part of the store's community and not just employees.

Almost all employees work full time. Paul says it takes 40 hours or so for an employee to catch on to the job, longer if he or she is part time. The initial cost of training an employee is about $300 in their time and his time and other small expenses. A part-time employee would never work out for the summer: the season would be over as he or she was just getting to know how to do the job. So the only part-time employees at the Café are exceptional locals who are in for the long term and have something special to offer.

Lesson #5: Make clear, consistent decisions about hiring and staffing. Make sure those decisions work for your company in all ways: meeting workflow demands, increasing retention, meeting quality requirements, reducing cost, meeting regulatory requirements, and more. Put those decisions into a policy manual and make sure that a practical, thorough up-to-date employee manual is available to all staff at all times.

See Chapter 16 for tools that will help you make good, lasting decisions that reduce hassle.

Paul needs to hire extra people for the summer tourist season. At first, this was a real challenge. Then Giedre, an exchange student from Eastern Europe, found Paul's store on the web and asked for a job. The schedule of exchange students worked better for the store than American students' schedules. Paul needs to keep extra people all the way into early September and most American students need to leave at the beginning of August. In addition, he found that the exchange students were very willing to learn and to work hard. Part of that is certainly economics—one of them earned as much money in a summer as her father earns in a year back home—but it is also a cultural attitude. Paul has had such good success with employees from Eastern Europe that he asked one of them to interview people back home and recommend them to him. As a result, he is getting a steady supply of good workers each summer.

In contrast, when he hired one local high school student, he told her that, as she learned various jobs around the Café, she would be able to get more responsibility. She didn't focus on learning and so she did a lot of scrubbing. After a month, she quit—via a text message, "I quit—I'm tired of cleaning up all the time." Paul says it's the first time he every had an employee quit by text message. But she had created the situation she didn't like by not trying to learn more of the job and then left the situation, missing out on the opportunity the Café was offering.

Hiring foreign students does create a problem with the language barrier. Paul hires only people who know English well enough to serve customers. Still, they sometimes stumble when learning new jobs. Paul solved this by having some come before the busy season and then help with training others in their native language. However, Paul is careful to ask them not to chat with one another in their own language in the store. That could disturb customers. And it is also better for the exchange students—it keeps them practicing their English.

Some of the people Paul hires as permanent employees leave because, after a time, they find that they are just not cut out for this kind of work. Others stay for a while and then grow on to other careers. The last six months have been particularly challenging. Paul and Susannah had a child last November and also wanted to focus more on planning for the store than working behind the counter, so they decided to share just one job slot. Then they opened their new store, so they needed twice as many employees. And a manager who had been with them for quite a while announced that she had gotten a job opportunity in her new career—but stayed on for two months more out of loyalty, to see that Front Porch Two got onto its feet before she left. Paul says, "It feels like, as soon as I hire one person, another one leaves. Actually, though, it's worked out OK, and we're ready for the summer."

Lesson #6: Finding good people is an ongoing challenge for any small business, especially one that is growing. Look for innovative ways—such as using the World Wide Web—to cultivate sources of good employees. Find good ways to find good people and keep doing it.

See Chapter 5 for innovative ways to solve problems using the internet.

Some of the staff who stay have a chance to grow. Some grow in their technical ability, becoming barristas—expert makers of high-quality coffee drinks. This requires a lot of practice—and may involve staying up late after you've tasted too many samples. Paul and Susannah have to be sure of an employee's ability to produce excellent beverages consistently before he or she can run the shop and serve as barrista. There are also management opportunities, such as running one of the cafés when Paul and Susannah are not there. In fact, creating a chance for employees to grow was one of the reasons for creating the second café.

Lesson #7: If you want your company to grow, plan for your employees to grow with you.

Share your dreams with your team. See Chapters 4, 10, and 22.

Improvements—Roasting and Going Nuts!

From 1999 through 2004, The Front Porch Café innovated and grew in a number of ways. One of the most critical and challenging changes was the decision Paul and Susannah made to roast their own coffee beans—artisan roasting, as it is called. The change was motivated out of the desire to be able to provide consistently high-quality coffee. In purchasing roasted coffee from wholesalers, a café is limited in its ability to ensure consistent quality. Wholesalers may lump together coffee from different plantations in a single roasting batch and the quality will vary by source and time of year. Also, one of the best roasters available is in Seattle and the coffee takes ten days to arrive. If it rains in Kill Devil Hills, the store can run out of coffee while waiting for more beans. And a regional roaster Paul used was not as consistent in quality.

However, Paul's main concern about doing his own roasting was also quality. If manufacturers couldn't always roast well, could he? Could he really become a true artisan of roasting? Answering that question took a lot of time and research. Here are some of the questions he sought answers for by talking to vendors and to other cafés that roasted their own:

▶ What roasting equipment is reliable and produces high-quality coffee?

▶ Can a small shop do its own roasting and make a consistent top-quality product?

▶ What are the critical success factors for artisan roasting?

▶ How much time and effort would it take to learn?

▶ How much would it cost to do it?

Over time, talking to many people, Paul gained confidence that artisan roasting was the way to go and that he could do it well. He learned from the successes of other stores, and their failures as well. For example, one store had a manager who took on the task of roasting and did very well. But, when he left, the roaster sat in the corner, unused.

Early on, he had a chance to buy a used roaster from a local company that was going out of business and save some money. But he looked at it, saw it was ancient, and figured that it would probably be very hard to maintain. Instead, he let go of the quick opportunity, and began to do real research into the best way to do it, instead of the cheapest.

So Paul chose an excellent roaster and became the chief artisan. He wrote a manual on using the roaster for their café. When Ashley, a staff member, expressed interest, Paul trained her to roast, as well. She added to the manual as they worked and then added roasting recipes for each coffee that they make. Now, Paul takes over when his roaster is away on vacation. He is considering training another apprentice. Also, the roaster recently went from operating about 20 hours a week—enough for the first café—to about 35 hours a week, supporting both cafés.

See Chapter 6 for how to write a good work plan.

Lesson #8: If you are going to change the way you produce your product, do a lot of research and learn all you need to know to be confident in the new process. Also make sure you make the right investment and take the time to do it well.

Lesson #9: Make sure the knowledge on how to run a business stays with the business. A business should never rely on the skill of just one employee—not even yourself. Make sure that each process is fully documented as we described in Chapter 4, so that, if a person leaves, someone with appropriate skills can be trained to do the job in a reasonable amount of time.

Becoming an artisan roaster brought some additional benefits to Paul and Susannah. Some were expected; others were not:

- The coffee is consistently fresh.
- They can sell the coffee in bags locally and over the Internet, which gives them some extra income.
- They are able to select coffees by plantation and season, knowing where the coffee came from by what was printed on the bag, rather than selecting by nation and having to trust that the roaster delivered the right product.
- They have come to know more about coffee growers, organic coffee, and fair trade.

Lesson #10: Becoming an expert has the advantage of offering new value, greater quality, and ways of keeping the business interesting, improving profit, and reducing cost.

See Chapter 8 for lessons on how to increase your expertise and work with experts.

Other new growth and changes at The Front Porch Café were easier and less fraught with risk than the decision to roast their own. When the storefront next door became available, they felt it was better to lease it than let it go to someone else. A friend in Michigan had a successful paint-your-own-pottery store running on a simple business model. Paul took the lease, set up the store, and had another money-maker plus some room to grow. An unexpected side benefit was that employees who were good with customers but not with coffee could run the pottery-painting studio, Glazin' Go Nuts, very well. And, of course, mothers watching their children paint pottery would probably want a cup of coffee. And when the coffee shop got crowded, which it does every morning, the overflow could use the seating in Glazin' Go Nuts. At this point, Paul's stores were serving families with children—up into the early grade school years—with pottery and adults with coffee. He added the Garden of Beadin' as another creative outlet to draw customers—particularly teenagers—into the store. At first, it cost little and was just run as a store-within-a-store inside the pottery shop. When the third store in the strip mall became available, Paul took that over and made the bead shop full-sized. Now, people of any age have a reason to stop by his stores on a rainy day.

Lesson #11: Expansion isn't for everyone, but if you see a simple opportunity with several advantages and you're sure you can handle it, grab it.

Front Porch Two: A Dream Coming True

For many people, opening one store is success enough. But Susannah likes to realize creative visions and Paul likes to face the challenges of growing. Once The Front Porch Café and its two sister stores were running well, they began to dream of a new café: The Front Porch Nags Head, only 12 minutes away. This dream was backed by sound business ideas:

▶ They could serve more customers. Having learned the local community, they knew that there were plenty of people who would stop by the new location who weren't coming to the first café.

▶ They could reduce overhead percentages. Management costs and fixed costs for everything from marketing to bookkeeping to roasting coffee would go up, but would not double, increasing the ratio of revenue to cost.

In addition to the dream and the hard-dollar value, there were several reasons that fell into soft-dollar value:

▶ They could provide an opportunity for their managers to grow more independent.

▶ They could express a new level of creativity in the design of the new store.

▶ They could step back to run the businesses and let managers take care of the stores.

The new store was being built to their specifications, so they had a chance to design, do architecture, and make it what they truly wanted it to be. They made the most of that opportunity, spending a lot of time at other stores and restaurants, learning what works and envisioning what they wanted. Ultimately, the new store was created with a global coffee theme from the world map etched into the concrete floor to the hand-painted coffee-bag national flags of coffee-producing nations hanging from the ceiling. The coffee roaster now sits inside an enclosed glass room at the entry to the store, drawing in customers, but with its noise and heat shielded from the shop, so it can run while the store is open.

Paul did make one mistake that, fortunately, didn't create too much trouble—though it might have. His architect asked him for a plan for the store. Paul knew what he wanted and drew a quick sketch. The architect failed to tell him that whatever he drew was going to be literally set in concrete and couldn't be changed. Paul didn't know how exactly things were being locked down. As a result, overall, Paul had what he wanted, but there were a few inches too little here and there. That may sound minor, until you are trying to fit a 48-inch bakery case into a 45-inch space, and they don't make 45-inch cases. It took Paul a fair bit of hunting and some extra expense to get the appropriate kitchen equipment to squeeze into some of the spaces.

Lesson #12: Pay attention to design and work it out in more detail than you might think you need to.

See Chapter 6 for how to prepare a good design.

The other challenge Paul ran into was construction delays. Some of those were caused by rain and storms, some by tradespeople who didn't want work Christmas week or when it got too cold, and some by delays in getting permits from the local government. Paul had hoped to open in February, in time to be ready for the Spring Break rush, but the store didn't open until the end of March. They lost some money there, but they had scheduled the opening well ahead of May, so that, even with delays, they were ready for busy season.

Lesson #13: Expect delays, especially when you are relying on a number of vendors, on getting permits, or on experts and dependent tasks. If you have a crucial opening date, aim to be up and running quite a bit earlier.

See Chapters 9 and 17 to manage risks and delays.

Paul made one other choice in planning the opening of the new store—one that seems to run against good project management practice but, in this case, was the right thing to do. He opened the new store with a new point-of-sale system, instead of duplicating the cash register at the old store. The new system is better—easier to use, which makes it easier to train new employees—but there was a pretty steep learning curve involved in setting it up, learning to use it, and being ready to teach others.

What Paul realized is that, if he prepared well, the best time to use the new system was at the new store when it first opened. Business would be very light because no one knew it was open; people weren't used to dropping in for coffee on that corner. Business was much lighter at the new store in the first few weeks than at the first store even during the slowest time of the year.

So Paul was actually able to set up, learn, and test his new cash register more easily at the new store than at any time at the old store. He prepared well and the new store is running well with the new point-of-sale system. He'll upgrade the old register at the first store after the summer, when business slows down.

Lesson #14: If you really know your business, you can combine projects for optimal results.

See Chapter 22 for how to organize many projects for your business.

Tips for Those Starting a Business

As I write Paul's story, I'm concerned that it all sounds too easy. The first six years of Paul's business—including moving into artisan coffee and opening up three additional businesses—have been easy enough to be enjoyable for Paul. But he is an exceptional person. Our point is that starting a business can be this easy and fun, but it often won't be. Paul has seen a number of stores and restaurants open and fail. To Paul, it was clear that many were headed for trouble before they even got started. Most new businesses fail within the first three years. Paul has some good ideas about why and some thoughts about whether it might be right for you and how to do it well.

▶ *Starting a business means spending your nest egg to buy yourself a job, then getting to work.* Paul has seen a number of people start restaurants thinking, "Wow! I'll get other people to work for me and I'll have a fun place to hang out with my friends." They usually go out of business quite fast. An owner who doesn't love to work isn't going to make much money. To put it another way, if you don't want to work, don't work for yourself.

▶ *The manager's salary will be your only income for quite a while.* If you hire a manager to do things for you, you won't make any money.

▶ *Really know and plan your business.* Only by really knowing your business can you know all the types of expertise you will need to run the business, succeed, and grow if you want to. Learn from experts and hire expertise where you aren't good enough to do it yourself. But you have to be expert in something and do that yourself or you won't be able to afford to make the business work. If you don't want to bring in your own expertise, take on challenges, and work hard, don't start a business.

- *Know what skills you will need.* Have those skills, be willing to learn them, or be willing to hire someone who can do them, in that order.

- *Be ready to be decisive.* Paul says, "Opening a new store is 1,000 decisions. You have to get efficient at them. The decisions have to be done to open the store. You can't vacillate. You make it and move on."

- *Know the real cost of your business.* This means being ready for expenses. It also means not being hoodwinked by someone who offers to do all your bookkeeping for $5,000 a year when you can get it done well for $300. There are plenty of people who will take your money and not deliver much in return.

- *Trust people, but verify their work anyway.* "Trust but verify" is the auditor's motto and it's a good one for the small businessperson as well. Paul cites a very successful, wealthy local restaurant owner who still closes out the cash register at each restaurant every night at 2 a.m. He has learned from experience that even trusted employees will be tempted to toss in cash from sales without ringing it up and then take it home at the end of the evening.

- *Be there.* At the beginning, be at the store day in and day out. Learn everything there is to know in your own experience. As you hire committed staff, write down what you know—or have them write it up as they learn it—and create efficient ways of transferring your skills to the company and your team.

Starting a business—or growing one from one store to two or in other ways—is fun and exciting. Planning before you do and following through with your team can really make it pay off.

Conclusion

When Paul and I finished talking, I asked him what he was thinking of doing next. Not surprisingly, he had his eyes open for new possibilities. Equally expected, he's being cautious.

There's a new mall complex going up about an hour away and the owner wants him to open a café. His research shows that the location is active only during the summer, so Paul would have to earn a full year's rent in three months. To make that work, the new location has to work for breakfast, lunch, and dinner. It might need to be a light restaurant with some good reason for people to come by and stay, not just a coffee shop. He's playing around with ideas, but he's not sure about the one-hour commute. He enjoys being able to go to all of his stores every day.

As usual, Paul is looking at every opportunity from every angle. I'm not sure what he'll do. But I'm sure he'll be up to something new the next time I get to the Outer Banks. If you can't stop by the beach, check out his café at www.frontporchcafe.net.

Chapter 22

Case Study: Planning a Year of Projects

O NE OF THE FUN THINGS ABOUT LEARNING, TEACHING, AND CON-
sulting is that I get to share everything I've learned with my
clients and see them succeed. I'd like to do the same for you.
My clients like to take on big challenges—so they need all the
project management they can get to make each project efficient and keep track of everything. With my help, they start every year from
the top down with strategic planning to set direction and program management to organize the year's projects.

A Strategic Plan Adds Flexibility

A strategic plan is the baseline for a company's year. When you have a plan,
you can either follow it or do something better. As a result, you're not locked
into the plan. Actually, the plan makes it easier to decide when *not* to do the
plan.

Here's an example of how this works for me. As I was finishing a big
project, I got an e-mail announcing that a former client was looking for help
at the beginning of a new, large project. It's the kind of work that I love to
do. But I'm already pretty busy and this client, being in government, has to

put the request out for competitive bid. So, I will need to decide if I want to take the time to go after the job.

That decision will be pretty easy because I already know what I will do if I *don't* do this new job. My strategic plan is laid out: I know what projects I will be working on, how busy I am, and how much money I will make if I don't take the new job. I have a basis for comparison.

So, now all I need to do is look at the new opportunity. My administrative assistant will put together all the information. We will compare the value of the new project against the value of the work I will give up to do it—an *opportunity cost analysis*. If the value of this new job is greater than the value of what I am already planning to do, then I'll put in the bid. In the analysis, I'll look at whether this job is aligned with how I want my company to grow and also at any risks related to the job—potential delays that would use up my time and so forth. If you make your own strategic plan—using the tools in this chapter—you'll be able to make big decisions easily, too.

A company without an annual plan is under more stress and at more risk. Decisions take longer to make and, without practice making strategic decisions, it is too easy to jump after something that looks good, but actually won't pay off.

What Is a Strategic Plan?

A company's strategic plan sets its direction and defines the context that then defines what projects will help the business succeed and grow. If your company doesn't already have a vision, mission, and values statement, I recommend that you read two books:

- ▶ *Built to Last: Successful Habits of Visionary Companies,* by James C. Collins and Jerry I. Porras (1997), which explains the value of a company defining an enduring vision, mission, and values and then developing a strategy, and gives specific instructions for creating a vision, mission, and values statement in Chapter 11.

- ▶ *The Seven Habits of Highly Effective People,* by Stephen R. Covey (1990), which can teach you how to create corporate and personal mission statements and can help you organize your work and time so that you can achieve your goals and lead others.

A company's vision, mission, and values statement should have one part that does not change and another part that changes in response to what our customers need. For example, Boeing will always build cutting-edge airplanes and spacecraft, but what defines "cutting edge" changes each decade. Also, in the first few years of strategic planning, we are still defining who we are and what the company stands for. So, we may revise and refine the plan.

My clients find that having a strategic plan with vision, mission, and values really helps, year after year. It allows us to do what we want to do: realize our dreams and solve our problems. Whether we want to grow the business, or work smarter and get some time off, the strategic plan is a tool that brings success to our businesses and balance to our lives. Strategic planning lets us consider creative ideas and new possibilities and then focus on the ones that matter most.

How to Plan Strategy Each Year

Each year, you can review and improve the permanent part of your strategic plan, the core vision, mission, and values. After the first few years, these are likely to become pretty stable. Then we focus on updating the mission or creating a new mission for the year. This mission is about goals of corporate growth and opportunity and about solutions to major problems. It also makes sense to review and revise your mission to customers. We all succeed by serving customers, but how will you serve them this year? If you discover you've gotten a new type of client or customer, is that a new direction or a temporary twist in the road? Strategic planning lets you make general plans into specific ones, and choose which trends to follow, and which ones to let go because there's something more valuable or more meaningful to do.

Some years, the strategic plan is about how to realize our dreams. Other years, it is about how to dig ourselves out of a deep hole we've dug ourselves into.

Strategic planning puts together two questions:

► What do I want to do this year?

► What is best for my business this year?

The answer to those questions are your company's projects for the year. Table 22-1 gives the process instructions for annual strategic planning.

Part of the work of creating a strategic plan should be on a retreat, but not all of it. Before the retreat, you should gather all the information you can and read and review everything. Also, don't assume you should go on retreat

Work Environment	Business owners or senior executives taking time aside for an annual strategic planning session in an organization that uses the *Get It Done Right!* method.
Input	• Prior year's strategic plan • Any reviews of major projects or work from the prior year • Corporate financial statements • List of customers and revenue per customer • Any documents describing business issues or problems • Any other documents you find valuable in assessing your business
Tools	• Large pads, paper, sticky notes • Word processing program • Spreadsheet program
Resources	Time aside from work
Techniques	• Methods in *Built to Last* by Collins and Porras and *The Seven Habits of Highly Effective People* by Covey • Methods in these process instructions
Process	1. Read last year's strategic plan 2. Ask yourself where you want to be in three to five years. Review the part of the plan that discussed that and update it. 3. Create a spreadsheet listing goals and actual results achieved. Look for major variances only. Don't worry about details such as whether the work was done on time or completely within budget. 4. For each major variance, note whether there was a conscious decision to cancel the project or if it just drifted out of sight or if you kept at it, but didn't finish. 5. For each realized goal, ask, "Is this something I want to do again this year?" 6. For each problem solved, ask, "Was this problem permanently solved? Could the solution apply more widely?" 7. For each cancelled or unfinished goal, ask, "Do I want to do this in the coming year?" 8. Based on your answers in 5, 6, and 7, write up a partial draft list of goals for the next year. 9. Look at your list of clients. Are there any you want to do more business with? Any you want to drop? Any types of clients—market segments—you want to pursue further? Add these ideas to your draft plan. 10. Step way back and listen to your dreams. Is there anything new and different you want to do? Add those to your draft plan. 11. Look at your input documents and talk with your team members. Do they have any dreams? Do they have any major problems that need solving? Add those opportunities and problems to your plan.

Table 22-1. Process instructions: annual revision of a strategic plan (continued on next page)

Process	12. Use the survey in Chapter 1 to create an updated list of problems and opportunities.
	13. Use all the material in Chapters 1-4 to organize your business and its programs.
	14. All of this is your draft plan. Now, you can use the techniques on brainstorming from Chapter 11 to organize the ideas.
	15. State items in the plan as goals.
	16. Organize those goals into groups, looking for the largest issues to be solved and looking for opportunities to align your business and align to your customers, as we discussed in Chapter 14.
	17. Define all of this into programs that serve customers for pay, develop new products, or improve operations.
	18. Figure out which programs add the greatest value.
	19. Decide how many programs you and your team can do this year.
	20. Include those programs in your plan.
	21. For each of those programs, define and prioritize the projects.
	22. In areas where you had an idea for a program, but you don't have the time and money to do it, see if there is a smaller project that will solve part of the problems.
	23. Throughout the whole document, make sure everything is clear, especially the goals.
	24. Share this with your team.
	25. Working with your team, schedule work and goals for each month of the year.
	26. Review and revise your strategic plan.
Output	A strategic plan that will guide your company for the year, realizing the greatest value and steering for success.

Table 22-1. Process instructions: annual revision of a strategic plan (continued)

alone. Maybe the whole company should go! And after the retreat, we take the plan to our team and, with our team, add details and build it into the schedule. Have every director or manager make his or her part work: get input from each one and have each one develop his or her own schedule for delivering the results that will make your company succeed.

Conclusion

Project management is about making dreams into reality, solving problems, and making money along the way. Give yourself time to dream. Then create a strategic plan that will focus the work of the year to make your dreams and your team's dreams real.

A strategic planning retreat is a time for reflection and learning. Don't make last year's mistakes again; learn from them.

Appendix

Forms
and Tools

FORMS MAKE IT REALLY EASY TO LEARN PROJECT MANAGEMENT, TO teach it to your team, and to save a lot of time keeping track of your projects. Forms scare some people. I suggest that you see them as friendly assistants. To plan your projects and keep everything under management, you need to answer a lot of questions and organize a lot of information. Wouldn't it be nice if you had an administrative assistant to remember all the right questions and things you should keep track of? Well, most of us can't afford that assistant, but forms are the next best thing. Think of each box on the form as a friendly reminder. Think of the whole form as a bunch of questions already organized for you. Each question is easy. Answer it, then the next one and then the next one. When you're all done, wow! your project is organized.

The forms and tools you see on the next several pages are just the tip of the iceberg. As a reader of *Project Management for Small Business Made Easy*, you get a lot more forms, tools, and free stuff at www.qualitytechnology.com/ DoneRight. In addition, those tools are editable, so you can change them, and so you can enter information right on your computer using Microsoft Word® or Microsoft Excel® and other programs. Page through these forms, use them, and then go online to get even more!

Questionnaire: Are You Ready to Learn PM?

This questionnaire will help you plan how to use this book well. It is based on Chapters 1 and 2.

Instructions: Write down your answers to the questions. Then go to the key (page 216) to interpret your answers and plan how you can best use this book.

1. Why did you pick up this book?

2. What are the biggest problems and challenges you face in your business? (List one to three.)
   - ▶
   - ▶
   - ▶

3. What are the biggest opportunities for you or your business right now? (List one to three.)
   - ▶
   - ▶
   - ▶

4. How much do you know about project management? (Pick one.)
   - ❑ Zip. I don't even know what a project is.
   - ❑ I know what a project is, but nothing about how to manage one.
   - ❑ I've got the basics down: goals, time, cost, planning—but I really don't know how to get a project done on time.
   - ❑ I can do a project myself, but I don't know how to lead a team.
   - ❑ I'm pretty good, but I want to be able to get projects done on time and within budget more often.
   - ❑ I'm a good—or great—project manager, and I'm looking to grow.

5. How important is learning to get jobs done on time to you and your business?
   - ❑ Crucial. Without it, I'm likely to lose my business.
   - ❑ Very important. I'm sure that this is where my company is stuck.
   - ❑ It matters a lot. The improvements would be a big help.
   - ❑ It can help. It's one of the things that we need.
   - ❑ Right now, there are other priorities, but I want to get a handle on this.

❑ I'm not sure.

❑ Actually, now that I think about it, I'll give the book to someone who needs it more than I do.

6. How much time do you have to read and *use* this book?

❑ Two or more hours per day: I'll make the time—I'm desperate.

❑ A few hours a week.

❑ I'll kind of read it around the corners, as I get time.

❑ I have to get some other things done first, and then I can put in some good time. But I'd like to get a handle on it now.

❑ Help! I'm so buried in work that I don't have time to learn how to do a better job!

7. What do you hope to learn from reading this book?

8. What do you hope to do differently after reading this book?

9. What projects would you like to get done soonest?

See Key on page 216.

Questionnaire Key

Check your answers against the following comments.

#1. *Always keep the answer to #1 in mind.* Stay connected with your reason for reading this book and applying what you learn from it. Read it aloud to yourself every time you open this book.

#2 and #3. *These lists of most important problems and opportunities form the list of projects you will do.* Solve big problems and help your business grow.

#4. *Plan your learning.* If you checked one of the first four boxes, then read all of *Project Management for Small Business Made Easy.* If you checked one of the last two, then skim the book and figure out what you most need to learn.

#5 and #6. *Make sure that the amount of time you're willing to invest matches your need.* If getting things done—or getting things done right—is your challenge, then the answer is here. But if you're overwhelmed, then you'll have to organize a bit and maybe set some other things aside to really use this book. But it will pay off. Every page offers quick tools that will save you time.

#7, #8, and #9. *These are your lists of goals.* Think of them as your finish line in a race. Keep your eye on the prize and check your progress. Whenever you finish reading a chapter, assess your progress against your answers to #7, #8, and #9 and set your direction toward your goals.

Set up Your Project Life Cycle

The tool on these two pages shows you how to apply the life cycle in Chapter 3 to every project. It applies to dreams and opportunities (see Chapter 4) and to problems and solutions (see Chapter 5).

	Gate 1: Start	Stage 1: Plan	Gate 2: Review the Plan	Stage 2: Do the Work	Gate 3: Check the Work	Stage 3: Deliver	Gate 4: Customer Delight
Project 1: Solving a Problem							
Work to be done	Name the problem. Launch the project.	Describe the problem. Define the solution.	Ensure the plan is complete and the project is worth doing.	Do the work to create the solution and test it.	Make sure the solution is good.	Deliver the solution. Train people as needed.	
Deliverables	Project charter	Project plan	Approved plan, schedule, and funds	Workable solution past initial tests	Solution ready to put into place	Solution in place, people working in a new way	Problem solved!
Project 2: Realizing an Opportunity							
Work to be done	Name the opportunity. Launch the project.	Describe the opportunity. Define the work to be done.	Make sure the plan is doable and the project is profitable.	Prepare for the event. Work on the campaign.	Final check before the event or launch.	Launch the campaign or run the event.	
Deliverables	Project charter	Goal statement and work plan	Work plan approved and team launched	Ready for opportunity (event, campaign)	Everything ready to go	Customer contact	Customer delight, company profit

Gate 1: Start	Stage 1: Plan	Gate 2: Review the Plan	Stage 2: Do the Work	Gate 3: Check the Work	Stage 3: Deliver	Gate 4: Customer Delight
Project 3: Developing a New Product or Service						
Work to be done						
Create a short description of the product. Launch the project.	Describe the product, its purpose, and its market. Plan how to develop, test, and produce the product.	Ensure development plan is complete and workable. Ensure product is good for company.	Develop and test the product. Develop and test the marketing plan.	Complete all product tests. Ensure the product is ready for market. Improve and approve the marketing plan.	Produce the product for sale. Perform marketing before launch date.	Introduce the product to market.
Deliverables						
Project charter	Product description, product development plan	Approval and funds to launch product development	Product ready for production, marketing plan ready for launch	Product enters production, marketing begins.	Product launch and beginning of sales	Customers delighted with the product

Five Ways to Make a List of Problems and Opportunities

For a full discussion of problems and opportunities, see Chapter 5. This tool will help you define the problems you can solve for your business.

There are many ways to make a list of problems and opportunities. Here are some of my favorites.

▶ Write down your worries. Then organize them into a bulleted list.

▶ Write down the things you'd like to do. Then organize them into a bulleted list.

▶ Bring your team together for a brainstorming session. Keep it practical. Sometimes, it's good to keep it specific, too. You can bring up a question such as "How can we sell more of Widget model 102?" or a more general question, such as "How can we improve the sales department?" The more experience your team has working together, the more general the question can be.

▶ Listen to your customers.

▶ Look at results. You can look at sales results, productivity reports, employee retention rates, or measures of productive work hours. Compare present results with past results. Are you where you want to be? If not, plan to get there. That's a project.

So, if you've followed the steps above, then you have goal—a problem you want to solve or an opportunity you want to seize. If not, go back and do one of them now! Why wait?

Priortizing Your Projects

There are many things we can do to make our business better, but we usually have time to do only one at a time. This tool will you apply Chapters 4 and 5 to your business most effectively. Read through this page, then use the form on the next page.

1. Make a list of problems and opportunities.
2. For each thing on your list, decide how important it is.
3. For each thing on your list, decide how urgent it is.
4. Organize the list using the Prioritized Projects form on the next page. (Instructions for using this tool are at the bottom of the form.)
5. Delegate anything you can to someone else.
6. Come up with a plan to take care of small things.
7. Pick one big thing that is important—and maybe urgent—and make that your next project.
8. Go through the planning steps in Chapters 4 and 5. If that project turns out to be too difficult to do now, go back to your list and pick a different problem or opportunity.

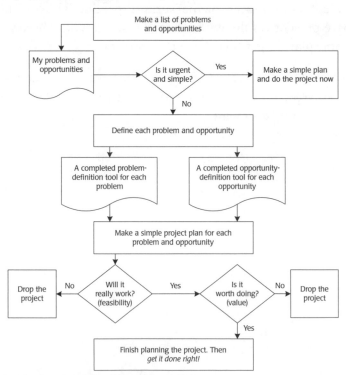

Selecting, prioritizing, and planning flowchart

Prioritized Projects

Company name:		
My name:		
Date:		
Urgent		**Important (but not due soon)**
Item	*Due date*	*Item*

Instructions:
1. Write each important item on a separate 3-by-5 card or sticky note.
2. Pick a date and put all items due before that date in one stack, called Urgent Items.
3. Organize the Urgent Items stack in order of due dates, with the item due first at the top.
4. Put all the other cards or notes in a separate stack, called Important Items.
5. Organize the Important Items stack in order of importance, with the most important item at the top.
6. List the Urgent Items in the left column of this table, from most to least, with the due date next to each item.
7. List the Important Items in the right column, from most to least.

Now, you're ready to turn each item—each problem or opportunity—into a project.

Problem-Definition Form

This form will help you apply Chapter 5 to any problem.

Name of the problem:
My name:
Date:
Company name:
Problem Description
Is there a crisis? Yes ___   No ___ (If yes, take immediate action, then come back to complete this form.)
What are the *symptoms*? (What tells me there is a problem? What do these symptoms tell me about the problem?)
What are the *causes* of the problem? (List one or more causes.)
What are the *consequences* of this problem? (What will happen if you do nothing? List one or more consequences.)

Opportunity-Definition Form

This form will help you apply Chapter 4 to any dream or opportunity.

The Question	How It Is Now (before they change)	How It Will Be After Opportunity Is Realized
The Results of the Opportunity This section describes business results before and after the change.		
Money		
Gross revenue		
Net revenue		
Customers		
Number of customers		
Type of customers		
Staff		
New staff		
People in different jobs		
Jobs that will be lost		
Products and Services		
New products or services		
Products or services that will be eliminated		
Changes or upgrades to products or services		
Tools and Equipment		
New tools and equipment		
Tools and equipment that will go away		
Tools and equipment that will be replaced or upgraded		
The New Way of Working This section describes our work process—how we do our work before and after the change.		
Executive Leadership Functions		
How will owners', executives', and senior managers' jobs change?		
Product and Service Development		
What will change in the ways we create our products and deliver our services?		

The Question	How It Is Now (before they change)	How It Will Be After Opportunity Is Realized
The Results of the Opportunity This section describes our work process—how we do our work before and after the change.		
Marketing		
What will change in the ways we market?		
Sales		
What will change in the ways we sell?		
Client Services and Customer Support		
What will change in the ways we serve clients and respond to customer support requests?		
Financial Operations		
What will change in the ways we do accounting and financial work?		
Research and Analysis		
What will change in the ways we do research and analysis?		

Simplest Project Plan

This tool is all you need to plan a small, simple, one-person project using Chapters 6 through 12. It can also be the first form you use to start planning a larger project.

Project name:
Company name:
Date:
Your name:
Why am I doing this project?
Where am I starting?
What is my goal?
Do I know my way around? (For the next three boxes, enter any questions you need to research or expertise you need to get.)
Business issues:
Project management issues:
Technical issues:
How will I do it? (Enter the major steps below.)

Instructions: Use this template for a quick, simple project that you can do alone or hand to someone who can do it in a few hours or a couple of days. Use one of the more complicated templates if you need to set deadlines, track cost, or assemble a team to do the work. If you like, you can start with this form and then shift to one of the bigger forms later.

1. Fill in the first four lines.
2. Answer "Why am I doing this project?" with business benefits and value, not technical features.
3. Answer "Where am I starting?" in terms of both the business situation and the technical situation.
4. Answer "What is my goal?" in terms of the business results, the new way of working, and the new technical solution.
5. Answer "Do I know my way around?" by considering whether you need some information (a map) or expert assistance (a guide) in relation to the business issues, the technical issues, or planning and managing the project.
6. After you do any research or get any expert assistance you need, write up the steps that take you from where you are now to your goal.
7. Review the whole project plan. Is everything in it clear? If someone else is going to work with you or do this work for you, is it clear to both of you? Could you put this in a drawer, take it out a week from now, and know exactly what to do? If not, revise it until it is completely clear.
8. Review the plan again. Is it complete? Does it solve every part of the problem? Does it cover every major step from the starting point to the goal? If not, add whatever is needed.
9. If you've reached this step, then your project is ready for evaluation so that you can decide whether or not this project will work and whether you want to do the project or not. This project is ready for two important questions: "Will This Really Work?" and "Is it Really Worth Doing?"
10. If you decide to do the project, follow the plan. If it is a simple, small project, you've done all the planning you need. If it is large or complicated, then you can build a more detailed project plan.

Net Revenue Is What Matters

These ideas will help you apply the material in Chapter 2 to your projects.

Net revenue is total (or gross) revenue—all the money coming in—minus total expenses—all the money that goes out. Ultimately, what is good for the business is an increase in net revenue. This is important to remember in three ways.

▶ *Increased revenue is worthless if it costs too much.* More money coming in doesn't necessarily mean more profit. We must increase revenue more than we increase expenses.

▶ *Cost cutting works only if it doesn't cut our revenue.* If we can cut costs while delivering the same product or service, with the same quality, in the same quantity, that's good. But if cutting costs means reducing quality and losing customers or not having enough product available and losing sales, then we lose revenue while reducing expenses and net revenue doesn't go up.

▶ *Sooner or later, vague ideas have to become hard dollars.* We must understand how and when good ideas will pay off. Here are some examples.

   – *Increased goodwill.* You might hear that, as a small business, if you help out with a volunteer or social benefit project in your town, people will appreciate you. That goodwill is very important. But goodwill becomes dollars only if it keeps or attracts customers. For example, you might donate to a local charity and issue a press release about the donation, so that customers link your charity with your business.

   – *Reduced cycle time.* The time it takes to bring a product to market, to close a sale, or to complete any other business activity is the *cycle time* of that process. In general, reduced cycle time is a good thing. It makes a company more flexible: if there's a change, it can respond faster. For example, if we automate our inventory and cash register system, we shorten cycle time on price changes. This allows us to adjust for inventory overstocks, competitors' price cuts, and changes in customer preferences and then lower prices for a sale more quickly. But, before installing the new system, we'll need to estimate exactly how this faster cycle time will increase net revenue. If we can estimate the change in dollars, that's a hard-dollar value. If we can only describe and estimate the benefit, that's soft-dollar value.

Is It Done?

Teach this to everyone on your team for project success. It will help with team-work and communications (Chapter 10) and keeping everything on track (Chapter 13).

Project management is about getting things done. In Chapter 1, I introduced the ideas of a task and a deliverable. I said that if you are doing one step and I'm doing the next step, then your output, your deliverable, is my input. If you don't do your job right, I can't start my job on time.

Now, I'm going to rant about this for just a minute. Why? Because I want to save you a lot of time and frustration.

Here's my rant: *project management won't work unless every team member understands tasks and deliverables.* You could spend thousands of dollars on project management training and get everyone professionally cer-tified, but if these really simple basics aren't a habit for everyone, then you're all spinning your wheels, wasting money and time, and getting nowhere. Here are the things everyone needs to understand:

▶ *Either it's done or it's not.* There is no such thing as "nearly done." That means nothing; it's like being "a little bit pregnant." If you're done, you have nothing else to do. You could put your deliverable on a shelf for six months and then a total stranger could pick it up and use it with no problems. When your task is done, you've delivered: you are not needed any more for that task; others can do it without you. If there is one tiny loose end, it isn't done and you say, "No, it's not done."

▶ *All deliverables should be written down clearly, so that everyone understands them.* In a small business, there is no room for "Oh, just one more thing" or "I thought that was what you wanted."

▶ *Plan your time, do what you say you're going to do, and get it done on time.* It takes a lot of practice to get good at this, but it pays off in credibility, respect, and the bottom line. In fact, it's worth working on every day, for the rest of our lives.

Consider writing a statement like this one and making sure everyone understands it. Help all members of your team see their strengths, weak-nesses, and next steps of growth in these basic skills.

Task-Description Form

Use this form and the instructions on the next page to delegate jobs to team members so that they can get it done right and contribute to project success.

Task name	What do we call this job?	
Project name	If this job is part of a larger project, what is the name of the project?	
Worker	Who will do the job?	
Person assigning task	Who is asking that the job be done?	
Output	What is the deliverable?	
Output	How do we make sure the deliverable works and the customer is satisfied?	
Output	Where do we record that the work was done?	
Output	What do we need to clean up when we're done?	
Output location	Where does the deliverable go when the job is done?	
Inputs	What do I need to start this job?	
Process	How do I do this job?	
Process	Are there any interim deliverables or status report times? When are they and what do I need to have ready for each?	
Process	What do I do if I can't get the job done or need help?	
Techniques	What are my instructions for this job? Is there a step-by-step method to follow?	
Tools	What equipment, tools, computer programs, and such do I use for this job?	
Resources	What else do I need to use for this job?	
Resources	How much time will it take to do this job?	
Resources	Is there anything else that costs money going into this job?	
Work environment	Where do I do this job?	
Work environment	What is around me when I do this job?	

All the Instructions for a Job

What are all the instructions a person needs to do a job? Let's assume that the job requires either no special training or special training that the person has already. What is required so that the person could walk in the first time, read the instructions, and do the job right?

- *A description of the starting point and the end point.* This would be the work request or project plan.

- *Any safety rules and procedures related to the environment and the tools.* Office safety procedures should be in place and equipment safety should be properly posted and included in training.

- *Information that makes the person comfortable and confident.* This is part of job orientation.

- *Step-by-step instructions.* For routine work, this is the SOP. For a project, this is the *work breakdown structure* and the activity list.

- *General ground rules, such as when and where to get help and report status.* These can be office guidelines or guidelines specific to the task.

- *The instructions that come with each tool.* That would include equipment operating instructions, computer program help files, and any useful manuals.

- *Special instructions on how to use the tool for this job in this work environment.* This part is often missed. Some programs—graphics programs such as Adobe PhotoShop® come to mind in particular— can do so many things in so many ways that it pays to have instructions on what part of the program to use in what ways to get particular results. Even in Microsoft Word®, it pays to have instructions in your own office for how to prepare document headers and footers, how to print letterhead, labels, and business cards, and similar tasks.

Multiple-Project Tracking Form

Use this form to keep track of the status of all your projects and tasks. Update it every time you get the status of each project using the tools in Chapter 13.

Worker:					
Updated:					
Projects					
Start Date	Due Date	Project	Deliverable	Link/Notes	Status
Small Tasks					
Start Date	Due Date	Project	Deliverable	Link/Notes	Status

Assigning Work

This tool will help you apply methods from Chapter 10, Teamwork and Communications.

When we're running a project, even a small one, we need to be able to assign work to other people. There's an art to that.

One time, I was teaching project management to a class of computer technical professionals. One of them said to me, "I don't understand how to manage people. I tell two computers to do the same thing and they both do exactly the same thing. But, just recently, I became a project leader. I told two people to do the same thing and they went and did completely different things."

I replied, "Welcome to the human race. People are like that; we're inherently unpredictable."

And that is the challenge of management. Our language—unlike computer languages—means different things to different people. Our memories—unlike computer memories—are not perfect. There is a real plus in each person's unique perspective and talents. But when it comes to assigning work, it can be difficult to make sure each person understands the job to be done.

All of the tools and templates we've introduced will help. The tools are even better if you teach people to write them and use them, not just to read them and follow the instructions. In addition, it helps to do these things when delegating work:

▶ *Let people know you want them to be proactive and self-managed.* You want them to own the work, to take responsibility for making sure it gets done right.

▶ *Let people know that you want them to stretch—a bit at a time.* Don't hand someone a job twice as big as he or she has ever done before and expect the person to succeed. But do ask everyone to do a good job, learn from mistakes, and get better and better as time goes on.

▶ *Support people in making mistakes—and learning from them.* You can't expect people to grow without making mistakes. And you can't expect people to make mistakes if they get yelled at, criticized, or warned they could lose their jobs when they do. Yes, mistakes cost a lot, but they are a part of doing business. It is our job to make sure that people can't make big mistakes. If we put someone in a position where he or she can make a big mistake, then we've given the wrong job to that person or put the wrong person on the job. We want people to be

231

able to stretch, take risks, and fail sometimes, as long as they learn from those mistakes, do better, and make different mistakes next time.

▶ *Make everything clear in writing.* That's the only fair way to check to see if the person did the job right.

▶ *Give people training when they need it.* Give people a chance to tell you they don't know how to do something, even if you think they should already know it. Then give them a way to learn it—spend a little time with them, let them do some self-guided study, send them to a training class, or just give them some time to figure it out. One great way to help people learn things is to have them write instructions for themselves. The instructions make the job clear and also give you a training tool for others.

▶ *Make sure they tell you that they understand the job.* When giving someone work, have him or her read the Task-Description Template. Or, perhaps even better, tell the person what you want, have him or her write it, and then rewrite it with him or her to fill in the details. Then have the person go over the questions in the template and make sure he or she understands the job in every way. Sure, it takes longer to get the job started. But it takes a lot less time to get it done.

▶ *If you give a person several jobs, make sure that the priority and due dates are clear.*

▶ *If jobs, priorities, or due dates change, make sure that the worker understands and that the latest instructions are written down.*

If we take these steps, we can delegate more and more work. Team members can become self-managed on larger and larger jobs. Then the whole team becomes more flexible. We solve more problems and everything runs better.

Building a Team To-Do List

This is an excellent way to do Work Breakdown Structuring. See Chapter 6 to learn more.

There is a very good reason to help team members build their to-do lists. With experience, a person can make a good list by himself or herself. But, until we've practiced it for quite a while, we tend to leave things out. Working in pairs, we can help each other. One person pictures the work he or she will do, while the other person asks questions and writes down the answers. This works well because the best way by far to make a good to-do list is through visualization—actually picturing the work. But it is very hard to visualize—a nonverbal, right-brained activity—and write—a verbal, left-brained activity—at the same time. So, the person who will do the work visualizes and the other person thinks logically, asking questions and writing down the results.

Here is the best way to do this:

1. In advance, set up the to-do list with initial situation, milestones, and room for steps in between.
2. Set up some uninterrupted time.
3. Ask the person to picture doing his or her work.
4. Ask him or her to name one thing he or she will do.
5. For each step named, ask, "If you were starting today, could you do that right now?"
6. If he or she says, "Yes," very clearly, write it at the top of the list. If he or she sounds uncertain, ask what he or she would do first. If he or she says, "No," ask, "What else would you have to do first?"
7. Write down the steps he or she would do first and then the step named.
8. For any big step, ask, "How would you do that?" Then, indented under the big step, write the smaller steps he or she would do to do the big step.
9. Walk through each step from the beginning—the initial situation—to the goal—the milestone. Ask him or her if, doing all those steps, he or she would reach the goal and complete the job. Add anything else that either of you think should be done.

Making Use of Expertise

Here we apply ideas from Chapters 10 and 11 to build a team that uses both our own staff and outside experts. Also see Chapter 21 for the story of how one small business owner does this really well.

Most people get locked into thinking that they have to figure everything out and do it themselves or they have to get someone else to do the job. That kind of thinking is bad for projects and bad for business. In reality, a little bit of the right expertise goes a long way to reducing project cost and preventing project disaster.

Projects are unique—they always contain something new. And the only way we can be confident that we know how to do something is if we've done it before, lots of times. So, on a project *there will always be some things the team doesn't know how to do*. The most important thing to do in project human resources management is to identify those things early and close the gap.

Of course, on most projects, the work is familiar. It is similar to what we've done before. It's just not quite the same. And it's those little differences that will trip us up every time.

What can we do about that? Well, think of it this way. An expert is someone who knows his or her way around so well that those little differences don't cause problems. He or she can see them ahead of time.

And there is always an expert available—*always*. We live in the information age. We complain about information overload. Make use of all that information. If you need to know something you don't know, you can count on this: *someone already knows it who probably has a book or a web site or will talk with you on the phone for free or for a small fee.*

Find that expertise. Do it now, during planning. It's a lot easier to find the information and close the gap now than in the middle of the project. That's when you find that the expert you want just went on vacation and his or her book just went out of print.

I'm hoping you'll take this advice. But many people won't. Why not? In a word—ego. Most people are locked into thinking in one of two ways:

▶ Some think, "I can't do this; I have to hire someone expensive."
  That's the sign of a weak ego, a person not confident of being able to learn and grow and solve the problems.

▶ Others think, "I have to do this all myself." That may be a person who overrates himself or herself, thinking no one can do the job, or a defense for a weak ego that needs to prove something by going it alone.

Well, sorry to be blunt, but get over yourself. You and your team can do the job, and yet you'll do it better—at lower cost and with lower risk of project failure—if you get the expert help you need early in the project.

Preparing a Communications Plan

This tool will give you what you need to develop a communications plan, as suggested in Chapters 6 and 10.

Work environment	• A project using the *Get It Done Right!* method, where the WBS and activity list are complete and planning is nearly complete
Input	• List of stakeholders • WBS and WBS dictionary • Activity list (or schedule, if it is ready) • List of milestones, stages, and gates • All other project plans
Tools	• Word processor
Resources	• Project manager's time—under half an hour for a small project, a few hours for a large one
Techniques	• Reading, thinking, and writing
Process	**Plan each gate review with these steps.** 1. Identify which project customers should be included in each gate review and which documents or components they need to approve. 2. Review the quality plan to define what constitutes a review of each document or component and ensure that all necessary inputs are available at the gate. 3. Plan to distribute all review documents at the opening of the gate review. 4. Schedule gate review meetings with team and customers. 5. Define all possible outputs of the gate review, including approval, minor and major rework requests, and calls for project cancellation. 6. Inform customers and technical staff of the gate review schedule, including educating them about the time that will be required of them. 7. Schedule the gate review, ensuring all information and people will be available. 8. Repeat steps 1-8 for each gate review and for final product delivery. 9. For final product delivery, add appropriate customer acceptance, project closure, and contract closeout activities. **Plan communications with peripheral stakeholders with these steps.** 10. Identify peripheral stakeholders and the project deliverables that each peripheral stakeholder needs to review and approve. 11. For each stakeholder, prepare a schedule of when he or she will review documents, test components, and perform final tests on the components that concern him or her. 12. Contact each stakeholder and identify his or her preferred forms of oral and written communication. 13. Include time for review and testing and, for each of these reviews and tests, steps for all possible outcomes (approval, change requests, or rejection). For the final test, include final customer acceptance sign-off.

Process	**Plan vertical communications with these steps.** 14. Identify the project sponsor, senior executives, and executive customers. 15. Ask each one how often and in what ways he or she wants to receive routine project status reports. 16. Explain project escalation procedures to each one and make sure that each one understands the project's need for prompt response to escalated issues. 17. Write up the vertical communications plan. 18. Identify any other special project communications needs. 19. Identify project stakeholders and team members in unusual situations, such as working for a vendor, working in a different department from most of the team, working at a different location, or having disabilities requiring special communications tools. 20. Determine which other team members each of these individuals needs to communicate with. 21. Contact all these individuals and define appropriate methods of communication. 22. Identify project team members with special technical needs, such as computer software or equipment that handles specialized data, graphics, or other media. 23. Prepare a section of the plan covering how all of these methods will be used. 24. Compile all of this into a project communications plan.
Output	A communications plan, including: • Agendas for gate review • Contact plans for peripheral stakeholders • Other communications guidelines as needed

Establishing a Status-Reporting Process

This tool provides step-by-step instructions for implementing the material in Chapter 13, Keeping Everything on Track.

Picture yourself and your team in the middle of the project. A week ago, you passed the planning gate, assigned all the members, and got them started. One week has gone by. What's going on? Have people gotten things done? Have they gotten stuck and not told you? Have they decided on a better way to do things and gone off in a totally different direction? Did they misunderstand you when you assigned the work, so that they aren't doing it yet or are doing something other than what you want? Or—and this is typical of a project in a small business—have they gotten caught up with routine work or customer requests or other problems and not done any work on the project at all? Remember the principle auditors follow: "Without attention, everything degenerates over time." All of the things I mentioned come up routinely. And the solution is to prepare, do, and follow through on the weekly planning meeting.

Here are the steps of gathering and using status information. Note that the weekly planning meeting—usually called a *status meeting*—is in the middle, covering steps 9 to 17.

1. Get *status information from every team member on every assigned task*. Get the status of each assigned task, including hours worked, percent complete, and any problems from each person working on the project. Also ask about the status of any risks related to their work and any new risks they see. You can gather this via a conversation, an e-mail inter-office memo, or data entered directly into a project management or timesheet information system. The time you collect this information is the *status date*.

2. *Enter the status information into your project management information system*. You may be working with Microsoft Project® or another package or simply using Word and Excel tables. Whatever your system, mark off the items that are complete, count up the hours, and update the project records of actual work done, actual time spent, and actual money spent.

3. *Define project status*. Know what is done and what is not, how much time has been spent, and how much money has been spent. This is the equivalent to being able to map your location when you are sailing so you can say, "We are here."

4. *Compare your status with your goal for the week.* Where did you plan to be at this point? Check the plan and see if each activity that was to be done by the status date has been done. Were any other activities done, indicating you are ahead of schedule? Have you spent more or less money and time than planned? Each difference between the plan and the actual situation is a *variance*.

5. *Evaluate each variance to see if it is significant.* Small variances—such as someone being one hour behind on a ten-hour job or an item budgeted for $100 costing $105.23—are just not worth worrying about. If you paid attention to them, you'd be micromanaging. That would hurt team morale and not be worth the time, energy, and headaches. So do something about only problems that are big enough to matter. A difference between planned WBS items (work) completed and actual work completed is a *scope variance*, a difference in effort (hours worked) is a *time variance*, and a difference in money spent is a *cost variance*. As you review the plan, also check the status of risk events and look for signs of new risks.

6. *Sort the significant variances into groups according to what you are going to do next.* Here are the groups:
   - *Items that involve just one team member and don't change scope, project, or schedule significantly.* If a person reported a problem and asked you for help or is repeatedly running late or doing poor-quality work, then resolve that with the person one on one before the staff meeting.
   - *Small but significant variances in scope, time, cost, or quality.* For these, propose a solution to the worker or get a proposal from the worker and then put the item on the agenda for the status meeting.
   - *Significant variances in work done, time, cost, or quality.* For these, you are going to have to pull the team together, evaluate the problem, and develop a solution.
   - *New risks.* Identify any new risks, update the risk plan, and prepare it for discussion at the weekly planning meeting.
   - *Proposed or approved changes to product scope.* Identify all issues that would actually change what you are making and prepare them for the project change management process.
   - *Other issues.* Review all nine project management areas and any other communication or conversations you've had and add them to the meeting agenda. On the agenda, specify whether you just want to be aware

of this issue, you want someone to plan action, or you are going to take action yourself.

7. *Help team members stay on track and on schedule.* Check each item of the types in the first two bullets under step six and address them with the team member before the weekly planning meeting.

8. *Prepare the agenda for the weekly planning meeting, including all items from step six.* For items from the first bullet, you can say something like "Joe is running a bit behind, but he'll take care of it." For each other item, define the gap and determine whether the team needs to monitor it or to take some action. If action is needed, put planning and assigning that action onto the meeting agenda.

9. *Hold the weekly planning meeting.* Cover all items on the agenda. Get everyone on the same page. Spend less time on smaller items and items with a clear solution. Spend more time on items that could really change the project plan. Make time for brainstorming on complex issues to define the problem clearly and come up with proposed solutions.

10. *Discuss scope issues.* Is work getting done on time? If not, why not and what can be done? Remember that there is no such thing as "almost done" and that when a person says a job is done, someone else can use that deliverable as input without needing an explanation or a fix.

11. *Discuss time and cost issues.* If the project, in general, is using more effort than expected or running behind schedule or spending too much money, bring that up with the team.

12. *Discuss quality issues.* If things are getting done, but not well, work will jam up at the review gate.

13. *Review the risk plan.* Check status on every risk. Introduce the new risks that were reported or that you learned about. Have the team suggest any possible new risks—a little proactive worry is good for a project. Cross off any risks you have gotten past and make sure that someone is watching or working on every current risk.

14. *Review other issues as needed.* If there are any issues of human resources, procurement, or anything else, now is the time to bring them up.

15. *Discuss whether the plan needs to be rebaselined.* If the project is running so far behind or over budget that it will not meet the gates, then you need a major revision to the schedule—a rebaselining. If you do, let the team

know and expect to spend some time during the week figuring out the best way to make the plan work.

16. *Discuss whether the scope or the whole project needs to be changed.* Work through the status of change requests and decide what needs to be done.

17. *Close the weekly status meeting.* Make sure that every item is assigned to someone on the team for some further monitoring, planning, or work.

18. *Follow up on routine items to keep on course with the baseline plan.* Take care of things and help any team members who need or want help.

19. *Keep monitoring and managing risks.*

20. *Follow up on rebaselining, if needed.* This will involve some time developing a new plan and schedule and some time meeting with people to figure out the best new plan and to come up with a permanent preventative solution for the root cause of the problem that forced a rebaselining.

21. *Follow up on project change management.* Approve or reject changes, inform people of the decisions, and rebaseline if needed.

That's a lot! Now you know why a project needs a manager!

Remember that, although I called this a weekly meeting, you may choose to track all of these items twice a week or daily if the project needs particularly close monitoring due to high risk or other complications.

A Status Meeting for a Team of One

Of course, in small businesses, we often do small projects. The project might be short—a few hours of work over a few days. And the team might be small—you may be the only person on the project, a team of one.

You should still gather status information, do status reporting, and take corrective action. When you are working alone, it is easy to keep going and think you're doing well when actually you've lost track of something or you're running behind and you don't know it. Sitting down and going through the 21 steps of status reporting and corrective action is as important for a team of one as it is for a team of 20.

Stopping Scope Creep

Here are some simple steps to solve the project of scope creep, as discussed in Chapter 14.

There are things we can do in planning and controlling a project to prevent scope creep and keep scope changes to a minimum. In planning:

- ▶ Define scope clearly and get approval from every stakeholder.
- ▶ Define scope in detail, including all requirements.
- ▶ Make sure everyone is on the same page with the same picture and that the picture is supported by precise written specifications.
- ▶ Teach the 1:10:100 rule to encourage a complete plan and few changes afterwards.

During the doing phase, through scope control:

- ▶ *Educate all team members* about the change control process and show them how to submit change requests. Ask that all requests include a justification.
- ▶ *Manage sources of change.* When a change request comes in, evaluate its cause. Does it indicate incomplete planning? A team member with a bright idea? A customer who thinks he or she can just ask for more? A customer who wants more and a too-customer-oriented team member? If the cause is any of these, then, aside from what you do with the one change request, bring the *source of change requests* under management.
- ▶ *Manage expectations by keeping in touch with the customers.* Keep the customers posted on progress, so that they stay focused in reality and don't start dreaming up new things for you to do for them.
- ▶ *Discuss scope change with your team members,* so they can help you keep it under control.
- ▶ *Bring every change request into the scope control process.* Don't miss anything and never ignore anyone. Respond to every change, even if your response is a firm, clear "No."

Index

About the Author

Sid Kemp, PMP, is a nationally recognized expert in project management, quality management, and strategic planning. The author of eight books, he brings the best practices of the *Fortune* 500, think tanks, and large government projects to small and medium-sized business. Sid has trained over 2,000 project managers. Learn more about Sid and his work as an author, consultant, trainer, and coach at **www.qualitytechnology.com**. Sid enjoys filling his web site with additional tools for his readers, meeting his readers over the web, and answering their questions.